Letters
from the
Light

Letters
from the
Light

An Afterlife Journal
from the Self-Lighted World

Written through the hand of Elsa Barker

With a Foreword and an Afterword by Kathy Hart

**BEYOND
WORDS**
Publishing
I N C

Beyond Words Publishing, Inc.
4443 NE Airport Road
Hillsboro, Oregon 97124-6074
503-693-8700
1-800-284-9673

Design: Principia Graphica
Typesetting: Typography Services

Printed in the United States of America
Distributed to the book trade by Publishers Group West

The corporate mission of Beyond Words Publishing, Inc.:
   Inspire to Integrity

Library of Congress Cataloging-in-Publication Data
Hatch, David Patterson, 1846–1912 (Spirit)
   [Letters from a living dead man]
   Letters from the light : an afterlife journal from the
self-lighted world / [channelled by] Elsa Barker ;
foreword and afterword by Kathy Hart.
      p.   cm.
   Originally published: Letters from a living dead man.
London : W. Rider, 1914.
   ISBN 1-885223-08-0 : $18.95
   1. Spirit writings. 2. Future life—Miscellanea. I. Barker,
Elsa, 1869–1954. II. Title.
   BF1301.B3   1995
   133.9′3—dc20   94-43637
                                                            CIP

The republication of these letters
is dedicated to all those
who are ready to enjoy the freedom
and unlimited potential of eternal life

TABLE
OF CONTENTS

TABLE OF CONTENTS

TABLE OF CONTENTS

F O R E W O R D

Certain precious books have changed my life. Few have done so more profoundly than this one.

As so often happens with valuable information, the book came to me when I most needed to read it. At the time, I was approaching forty and going through a period of disillusionment that was wracking me both emotionally and physically. A dear friend, Laura Riley, sympathizing with my precarious state, loaned me the book in a particularly dire hour of need. I credit her and the author for significantly altering the course of my life.

The story of how the book reached me is as uncanny as how it came to be written in the first place. Phil Ginolfi was seventeen years old in 1965 when he came across the book in a Victorian-building-turned-used-bookstore in Stamford, Connecticut. "The book made a tremendous impact on me," Phil told me. "It became one of my most treasured possessions." Then, in 1972, when Phil was living in Darian, a longtime friend visiting from Miami asked to borrow the book. "I was reluctant to part with it, but since he was a long and trusted friend, I couldn't refuse him." The friend took the book with him back to Miami. Three months later, his car was stolen, with the book in the trunk.

Four years passed. Phil was driving through Northhampton, Massachusetts, when he noticed a Victorian-house-turned-used-bookstore. "It had the same feeling about it as the bookstore in Stamford," Phil explained, "so I decided to go in. I walked in the door and straight down the hallway. I didn't stop to ask directions; I just went down the hall, turned a corner into a small back room, lifted my arm and reached out for a book. It was the same copy of *Letters* that had been stolen four years earlier in Miami."

That was in 1976. "I knew I had been directed to have that book, but I didn't understand why," Phil went on. "Several years later I moved to California, where I met a woman named Laura Riley. Eventually she read the book, and later asked if she could loan it to a friend—you. After you read the book and told me you wanted to republish it, I knew why I had found the book—twice—and why I had held on to it all those years."

Phil was seventeen when he first read *Letters*. I was nearly forty. I didn't believe in reincarnation; I didn't believe in God or any kind of higher intelligence; and despite my protestations to the contrary, I feared death deeply. Certainly I did not believe that the dead could speak through the living.

What I find most remarkable about these letters is that one does not have to believe in channeling to appreciate the wisdom so eloquently put forth by the writer—whomever he or she may be. Whether they are the words of a deceased judge speaking through Elsa Barker, or whether they came from Elsa Barker's subconscious or from another source altogether, they provide an inspiring perspective on death *and* on life that both mitigates our fears of dying and impels us to live to the fullest.

Immediately after reading the book, I had two responses: I wanted everyone I knew to read it, and I wanted a copy of my own. This second ambition, I realized, would be no easy one to achieve. *Letters* was originally published in 1914; surely it was long out of print. I wrote to an out-of-print-book-finding service in New Jersey. After six months, the company wrote to say it had found a copy.

When the book arrived, however, it turned out to be not the one I had ordered but a sequel. In the second volume of *Letters*, published in 1915, the deceased correspondent, referred to only as "X" in the original volume, is identified, and there is included in the book a photograph of the Honorable Judge David Patterson Hatch.

•

(See the Afterword on pages 269–76 for photographs and biographical information on Judge Hatch and Elsa Barker.)

Over the next several years, I made various attempts to find a publisher for the letters, without success. Then in 1987, I met Michael MacMacha and had my first experience with a living "channel." Michael gave voice to a spiritual grande dame named Evangeline whose wise counsel on many subjects impressed me greatly. I decided to have a private consultation with Michael/ Evangeline, to ask about the republication of *Letters*. Evangeline's response was direct:

"I know of this book," she said. "It's a very im-
portant book, and it should be republished. And you will be the one to have it republished. But now is not the time. There are many channeled books coming out right now, and not all of them are genuine. Wait a while. You'll know when the time is right, because it will happen easily."

I was with my friend and mentor Arnold Patent at the American Booksellers convention in Los Angeles in May of 1994 when I met Cynthia Black and Richard Cohn, owners of Beyond Words Publishing. When they agreed to republish Arnold's books, I asked them if they would be interested in *Letters*. After reading the book, they said yes, and the republication process has been happening easily ever since.

•

Except for the title, the book remains essentially the same as the original 1914 edition. I used American rather than British spellings; I omitted one short letter in the beginning whose subject matter was more clearly and elaborately explained in a later letter; I deleted several brief passages that seemed to me to obstruct the flow of the book; and I changed a few words whose connotations today mean something slightly different from what they implied more than eighty years ago. As a professional editor for many years, I am confident I would have the approval of Judge Hatch and Elsa Barker in making these minor modifications.

My purpose in republishing *Letters* is perfectly reflected by Ms. Barker in her introduction to the book. She writes: "The effect of these letters on me personally has been to remove entirely any fear of death which I may ever have had, to strengthen my belief in immortality, to make the life beyond the grave as real and vital as the life here in the sunshine. If they can give even to one other person the sense of exultant immortality which they have given to me, I shall feel repaid for my labor."

This book is indeed a treasure. I sincerely hope you enjoy it.

Kathy Hart
San Francisco, 1995

INTRODUCTION

One night last year in Paris I was strongly impelled to take up a pencil and write, though what I was to write about I had no idea. Yielding to the impulse, my hand was seized as if from the outside, and a remarkable message of a personal nature came, followed by the signature "X."

The purport of the message was clear, but the signature puzzled me.

The following day I showed this writing to a friend, asking her if she had any idea who "X" was.

"Why," she replied, "don't you know that that is what we always call Mr. —— ?"

I did not know.

Now, Mr. —— was six thousand miles from Paris, and, as we supposed, in the land of the living. But a day or two later a letter came to me from America, stating that Mr. —— had died in the western part of the United States, a few days before I received in Paris the automatic message signed "X."

•

So far as I know, I was the first person in Europe to be informed of his death, and I immediately called on my friend to tell her that "X" had passed out. She did not seem surprised, and told me that she had felt certain of it some days before, when I had shown her the "X" letter, though she had not said so at the time.

Naturally I was impressed by this extraordinary incident.

Soon after my receipt of the letter from America stating that Mr. —— was dead, I was sitting in the evening with the friend who had told me who "X" was, and she asked me if I would not let him write again—if he could.

I consented, more to please my friend than from any personal interest, and the message beginning, "I am here, make no mistake," came through my hand. It came with breaks and pauses between the sentences, with large and badly formed letters, but quite automatically, as in the first instance. The force used on this occasion was such that my right hand and arm were lame the following day.

Several letters signed "X" were automatically written during the next few weeks; but, instead of becoming enthusiastic, I developed a strong disinclination for this manner of writing, and was only persuaded to continue it through the arguments of my friend that if "X" really wished to communicate with the world, I was highly privileged in being able to help him.

"X" was not an ordinary person. He was a well-known lawyer nearly seventy years of age, a profound student of philosophy, a writer of books, a man whose pure ideals and enthusiasms were an inspiration to everyone who knew him. His home was far from mine, and I had seen him only at long intervals. So far as I remember, we had never discussed the question of postmortem consciousness.

Gradually, as I conquered my strong prejudice against automatic writing, I became interested in the things which "X" told me about the life beyond the grave. I had read practically nothing on the subject, not even the popular *Letters from Julia*, so I had no preconceived ideas.

3

The messages continued to come. After a while there was no more lameness of the hand and arm, and the form of the writing became less irregular, though it was never very legible.

For a time the letters were written in the presence of my friend; then "X" began to come always when I was alone. He wrote either in Paris or in London, as I went back and forth between those two cities. Sometimes he would come several times a week; again, nearly a month would elapse without my feeling his presence. I never called him, nor did I think much about him between his visits. During most of the time my pen and my thoughts were occupied with other matters.

While writing these letters I was generally in a state of semi-consciousness, so that, until I read the message over afterwards, I had only a vague idea of what it contained. In a few instances I was so near unconsciousness that as I laid down the pencil, I had not the remotest idea of what I had written; but this did not often happen.

When it was first suggested that these letters should be published with an introduction by me, I did not take very enthusiastically to the idea. Being the author of several books, more or less well known, I had my little vanity as to the stability of my literary reputation. I did not wish to be known as an eccentric, a "freak." But I consented to write an introduction stating that the letters were automatically written in my presence, which would have been the truth, though not all the truth. This satisfied my friend; but as time went on, it did not satisfy me. It seemed not quite sincere.

I argued the matter out with myself. If, I said, I publish these letters without a personal introduction, they will be taken for a work of fiction, of imagination, and the remarkable statements they contain will thus lose all their force as convincing arguments for the truth of a hereafter. If

INTRODUCTION

I write an introduction stating that they came by supposedly automatic writing in my presence, the question will naturally arise as to whose hand they came through, and I shall be forced to evasion. But if I frankly acknowledge that they came through my own hand, and state the facts exactly as they are, only two hypotheses will be open: first, that they are genuine communications from the disembodied entity; second, that they are lucubrations of my own subconscious mind. But this latter hypothesis does not explain the first letter signed "X," which came before I knew that my friend was dead; does not explain it unless it be assumed ___ subconscious mind of each person ___ ich

case, why should

out upon a long

on a premise

to it by my ow

other person?

That anyo

deceit and r

not then and

having other

and fiction.

The letters

before this que

decided that if

should publish th

stating the exact circumstances of their reception by me.

The actual writing covered a period of more than eleven months. Then came the question of editing. What should I leave out? What should I include? I determined to leave out nothing except personal references to "X's" private affairs, to mine, and to those of his friends. I have not added anything. Occasionally, when "X's" literary style was clumsy, I have reconstructed a sentence or cut out a repetition; but I have taken far less liberty than I used, as an editor, to take with ordinary manuscripts submitted to me for correction.

6

So   colloquial; sometimes

               or American slang.

               bject to another,

               ondence, going

               out a connect-

               relative to the

               ntrary to the

               These state-

               . Many of his

               quite new to

               eir profundity

               or the publication

               ably an interesting

document, whatever their source may be, and I give them to the world with no more fear than when I gave my hand to "X" in the writing of them.

If anyone asks the question, What do I myself think as to whether these letters are genuine communications from the invisible world, I should answer that I believe they are. In the personal and suppressed portions, reference was often made to past events and to possessions of which I had no knowledge, and these references were verified. This leaves untouched the favorite telepathic theory of the psychologists. But if these letters were telepathed to me, by whom were they telepathed? Not by my friend who was present at the writing of many of them, for their contents were as much a surprise to her as to me.

I wish, however, to state that I make no scientific claims about this book, for science demands tests and proofs. Save for the first letter signed "X" before I knew that Mr. —— was dead, or knew who "X" was, the book was not written under "test conditions," as the psychologists understand the term. As evidence of a soul's survival after bodily death, it must be accepted or rejected by each individual according to his or her temperament, experience, and inner conviction as to the truth of its contents.

Introduction

In the absence of "X" and without some other entity on the invisible side of Nature in whom I had a like degree of confidence, I could not produce another document of this kind. Against indiscriminate mediumship I have still a strong and ineradicable prejudice, for I recognize its dangers both of obsession and deception. But for my faith in "X" and the faith of my Paris friend in me, this book could never have been. Doubt of the invisible author or of the visible medium would probably have paralyzed both, for the purposes of this writing.

The effect of these letters on me personally has been to remove entirely any fear of death which I may ever have had, to strengthen my belief in immortality, to make the life beyond the grave as real and vital as the life here in the sunshine. If they can give even to one other person the sense of exultant immortality which they have given to me, I shall feel repaid for my labor.

To those who may feel inclined to blame me for publishing such a book, I can only say that I have always tried to give my best to the world, and perhaps these letters are one of the best things that I have to give.

Elsa Barker
London, 1913

L E T T E R

I

THE RETURN

I am here, make no mistake.

It was I who spoke before, and I now speak again.

I have had a wonderful experience. Much that I had forgotten I can now remember. What has happened was for the best; it was inevitable.

I can see you, though not very distinctly.

I found almost no darkness. The light here is wonderful, far more wonderful than the sunlight of the South.

No, I cannot yet see my way very well around Paris; everything is different. It is probably by reason of your own vitality that I am able to see you at this moment.

●

L E T T E R

2

Tell No Man

I am opposite to you now in actual space; that is, I am directly in front of you, resting on something which is probably a couch or divan.

It is easier to come to you after dark.

I remembered on going out that you might be able to let me speak through your hand.

I am already stronger. It is nothing to fear— this change of condition.

I cannot tell you yet how long I was silent. It did not seem long.

It was I who signed "X." The Teacher helped me to make the connection.

You had better tell no one for a while, except ——, that I have come, as I do not want any obstructions to my coming when and where I will. Lend me your hand sometimes; I will not misuse it.

I am going to stay out here until I am ready to come back with power. Watch for me, but not yet.

•

Things seem easier to me now than they have seemed for a long time. I carry less weight. I could have held on longer in the body, but it did not seem worth the effort.

I have seen the Teacher. He is near. His attitude to me is very comforting.

But I would like to go now. Good night.

LETTER
3

A Cloud on the Mirror

When you respond to my call, wipe clean your mind as a child wipes its slate when ready for a new maxim or example by its teacher. Your lightest personal thought or fancy may be as a cloud upon a mirror, blurring the reflection.

You can receive letters by this means, provided your mind does not begin to work independently, to question in the midst of the writing. When this occurs, you suddenly become positive instead of negative, as if the receiving instrument in a telegraph office should begin to send a message of its own.

There was one night when I called and you would not let me in. Was that kind?

But I am not reproaching you. I shall come again and again, until my work is done.

I will come to you in a dream before long, and will show you many things.

•

L E T T E R
4

THE PROMISE OF THINGS UNTOLD

After a time I will share with you certain knowledge that I have gained since coming out. I have learned here the reason for many psychic things which formerly puzzled me.

I see the past now as through an open window. I see the road by which I have come, and can map out the road by which I mean to go.

Everything seems easy now. I could do twice as much work as I do—I feel so strong.

As yet I have not settled down anywhere, but am moving about as the fancy takes me; that is what I always dreamed of doing while in the body, and never could make possible.

Do not fear death; but stay on earth as long as you can. Notwithstanding the companionship I have here, I sometimes regret my failure in holding on to the world. But regrets have less weight on this side—like our bodies.

Everything is well with me.

I will tell you things that have never been told.

LETTER

5

THE WAND OF WILL

Not yet do you grasp the full mystery of *will*.
It can make of you anything you choose, within
the limit of your unit energy, for everything is
either active or potential in the unit of force
which is man.

The difference between a painter and a musi-
cian, or between a poet and a novelist, is not a
difference of qualities in the entity itself; for each
unit contains everything *except quantity*, and
thus has the possibilities of development along
any line chosen by its will. The choice may
have been made ages ago. It takes a long time,
often many lives, to evolve an art or a faculty for
one particular kind of work in preference to all
others. Concentration is the secret of power, here
as elsewhere.

As to the use of willpower in your present
everyday problems, there are two ways of using
the will. One may concentrate upon a definite
plan, and bring it into effect or not according to

the amount of force at one's disposal; or one may will that the best and highest and wisest plan possible shall be demonstrated by the subconscious forces in the self and in other selves. The latter is a commanding of all environment for a special purpose, instead of commanding, or attempting to command, a fragment of it.

In this communion between the outer and inner worlds, you in the outer world are apt to think that we in ours know everything. You expect us to prophesy like fortune-tellers, and to keep you informed of what is passing on the other side of the globe. Sometimes we can; generally we cannot.

After a while I may be able to enter your mind as a Master does, and to know all the antecedent thoughts and plans in it; but now I cannot always do so.

I am learning all the time. The Teacher is very active in helping me.

When I am absolutely certain of my hold upon your hand, I shall have much to say about the life out here.

LETTER
6

A Light Behind the Veil

Make an opening for me sometimes in the veil of dense matter that shuts you from my eyes. I see you often as a spot of vivid light, and that is probably when your soul is active with feeling or your mind keen with thought.

I can read your thoughts occasionally, but not always. Often I try to draw near, and cannot find you. You could not always find me, perhaps, should you come out here.

Sometimes I am all alone; sometimes I am with others.

Strange, but I seem to myself to have quite a substantial body now, though at first my arms and legs seemed sprawling in all directions.

As a rule, I do not walk about as formerly, nor do I fly exactly, for I have never had wings; but I manage to get over space with incredible rapidity. Sometimes, though, I walk.

Now, I want you to do me a favor. You know what a difficult job I often had to keep things

•

going, yet I kept them going. Don't you get discouraged about the material wherewithal for your work. Work right ahead, as if the supply were there, and it will be there. You can demonstrate it in one way or another. Do not feel weak or uncertain, for when you do you drag me back to earth by force of sympathy. It is as bad as grieving for the dead.

LETTER
7

The Iron Grip of Matter

To a man dwelling in the "invisible" there comes a sudden memory of earth.

"Oh!" he says. "The world is going on without me. What am I missing?"

It seems almost an impertinence on the part of the world to go on without him. He becomes agitated. He is sure that he is behind the times, left out, left over.

He looks about him, and sees only the tranquil fields of the fourth dimension. Oh, for the iron grip of matter once more! To hold something in taut hands!

Perhaps the mood passes, but one day it returns with redoubled force. He must get out of the tenuous environment into the forcibly resistant world of dense matter. But how?

Ah, he remembers! All action comes from memory. It would be a reckless experiment had he not done it before.

•

He closes his eyes, reversing himself in the invisible. He is drawn to human life, to human beings in the intense vibration of union. There is sympathy here—perhaps the sympathy of past experience with the souls of those whom he now contacts, perhaps only sympathy of mood or imagination. Be that as it may, he lets go his hold upon freedom and triumphantly loses himself in the lives of human beings.

After a time he awakes, to look with bewildered eyes upon green fields and the round, solid faces of men and women. Sometimes he weeps, and wishes himself back. If he becomes discouraged, he may return—only to begin the weary quest of matter all over again.

If he is strong and stubborn, he remains and grows into a man. He may even persuade himself that the former life in tenuous substance was only a dream, for in dream he returns to it, and the dream haunts him and spoils his enjoyment of matter.

After years enough he grows weary of the material struggle; his energy is exhausted. He sinks back into the arms of the unseen, and men say again with bated breath that he is dead.

But he is not dead. He has only returned whence he came.

19

•

LETTER
8

WHERE SOULS GO UP AND DOWN

My friend, there is nothing to fear in death. It is no harder than a trip to a foreign country—the first trip—to one who has grown oldish and settled in the habits of his own more or less narrow corner of the world.

When a man comes out here, the strangers whom he meets seem no more strange than the foreign peoples seem to one who first goes among them. He does not always understand them; there, again, his experience is like a sojourn in a foreign country. Then, after a while, he begins to make friendly advances and to smile with the eyes. The question, "Where are you from?" meets with a similar response to that on earth. One is from California, another is from Boston, another is from London. This is when we meet on the highroads of travel; for there are lanes of travel over here, where the souls go up and down as on the earth. Such a road is generally the most direct line between two great

•

centers; but it is never on the line of a railway. There would be too much noise. We can hear sounds made on the earth. There is a certain shock to the etheric ear which carries the vibration of sound to us.

Sometimes one settles down for a long time in one place. I visited an old home in the State of Maine, where a man on this side of life had been stopping for I do not know how many years. He told me that the children had grown to be men and women, and that a colt to which he became attached when he first came out had grown into a horse and had died of old age.

There are sluggards and dull people here, as with you. There are also brilliant and magnetic people, whose very presence is rejuvenating.

It seems almost absurd to say that we wear clothes, the same as you do; but we do not seem to need so many. I have not seen any trunks; but then I have been here only a short time.

Heat and cold do not matter much to me now, though I remember at first being rather uncomfortable by reason of the cold. But that is past.

21

L E T T E R

9

A RENDEZVOUS IN THE
FOURTH DIMENSION

You can do so much for me by lending me
your hand occasionally, that I wonder why you
shrink from it.

This philosophy will go on being taught in
the world and all over the world. Only a few,
perhaps, will reach the deeps of it in this life; but
a seed sown today may bear fruit long hence.
Somewhere I have read that grains of wheat
which had been buried with mummies for two or
three thousand years had sprouted when placed
in good soil in our own day. It is so with a philosophic seed.

It has been said that he is a fool who works
for philosophy instead of making philosophy
work for him; but a man cannot give to the
world even a little of a true philosophy without
reaping sevenfold himself, and you know the
Biblical quotation which ends, "and in the world
to come eternal life." To get, one must give. That
is the Law.

•

I can tell you many things about the life out here which may be of use to others when they make the great change. Almost everyone brings memory over with him. The men and women I have met and communed with have had more or less vivid recollection of their earth life—that is, most of them.

I met one man who refused to speak of the earth, and was always talking about "going on." I reminded him that if he went on far enough, he would come back to the place from which he started.

You have been curious, perhaps, as to what we eat and drink, if anything. We certainly are nourished, and we seem to absorb much water. You also should drink plenty of water. It feeds the astral body. I do not think that a very dry body would ever have enough astral vitality to lend a hand to a soul on this plane of life, as you are doing now. There is much moisture in our bodies over here. Perhaps that is one reason why contact with a so-called spirit sometimes gives warm-blooded persons a sense of cold, and they shiver.

It is something of an effort on my part also to write like this, but it seems to be worthwhile.

I come to the place where I feel that you are. I can see you better than most others. Then I reverse; that is, instead of going in, as I used to do, I go out with great force and in your direction. I take possession of you by a strong propulsive effort.

Sometimes the writing may stop suddenly in the midst of a sentence. That happens when I am not properly focused. You may have noticed when reversing and shutting away the outside world that a sudden noise, or maybe a wandering thought, would bring you right out again. It is so here.

Now, about this element in which we live. It undoubtedly has a place in space, for it is all around the earth. Yes, every tree visible has its invisible counterpart. When you, before sleep, come out consciously into this world, you see things that exist, or have existed, in the material world also. You cannot see anything in this world which has not a physical counterpart in the other. There are, of course, thought-pictures, imaginary pictures; but to see imaginatively is not to see on the astral plane—not by any means. The things you see before going to sleep have real existence, and by changing your rate of vibration you come out into this world—or rather you go back into it, for you have to go in, in order to come out.

Imagination has great power. If you make a picture in your mind, the vibrations of the body may adjust to it if the will is directed that way, as in thoughts of health or sickness.

It might be well as an experiment, when you want to come out here, to choose a certain symbol and hold it before your eyes. I do not say that it would help to change the vibration, but it might.

I wonder if you could see me if just before falling asleep you should come out here with that thought and that desire dominant in your mind?

I am strong today, because I have been long with one who is stronger; and if you want to make the experiment of trying to find me this night, I may be able to help you better than at another time.

There is so much to say, and I can seldom talk with you. If you were differently situated and quite free from other things, I could perhaps come often. I am learning much that I should like to give you.

For instance, I think I can show you how to come out here at will, as the Masters do constantly.

At first I took only your arm to write with, but now I get a better hold of the psychic organization. I saw that I was not working in the best way, that there was a waste somewhere, so I asked the Teacher for instruction in the matter.

•

By this new method you will not feel so tired afterwards, nor shall I.

I am going now, and will try to meet you in a few minutes. If the experiment should fail, do not be discouraged; but try again some other time. You will know me all right, if you do see me.

L E T T E R
IO

The Boy—Lionel

You will be interested to know that there are people out here, as on earth, who devote themselves to the welfare of others.

There is even a large organization of souls who call themselves a League. Their special work is to take hold of those who have just come out, helping them to find themselves and to adjust to the new conditions. There are both men and women in this League. They have done good service. They work on a little—I do not want to say higher plane than the Salvation Army, but rather a more intellectual plane. They help both children and adults.

It is interesting about the children. I have not had time yet to observe all these things for myself; but one of the League workers tells me that it is easier for children to adjust themselves to the changed life than it is for grown persons. Very old people are inclined to sleep a good deal, while children come out with great energy, and bring with them the same curiosity that they had in earth life. There are no violent changes. The little ones grow up, it is said, about as gradually and imperceptibly as they would have grown on earth. The tendency is to fulfill the normal rhythm, though there are instances where the soul goes back very soon, with little rest. That would be a soul with great curiosity and strong desires.

The children are so charming! One young boy is with me often; he calls me Father, and seems to enjoy my society. He would be, I should think, about thirteen years old, and he has been out here some time. He could not tell me just how long; but I will ask him if he remembers the year, the calendar year, in which he came out.

It is not true that we cannot keep our thoughts to ourselves if we are careful to do so. We can guard our secrets, if we know how. That is done by suggestion, or laying a spell. It is, though, much easier here than on earth to read the minds of others.

We seem to communicate with one another in about the same way that you do; but I find, as time goes by, that I converse more and more by powerful and projected thought than by the moving of the lips. At first I always opened my mouth when I had anything to say; it is easier now not to do so, though I sometimes do it still by force of habit. When a man has recently come out, he does not understand another unless he really speaks; that is, I suppose, before he has learned that he also can talk without using much breath.

But I was telling you about the boy. He is all interest in regard to certain things I have told him about the earth—especially airplanes, which were not yet very practicable when he came out. He wants to go back and fly in an airplane. I tell him that he can fly here without one, but that does not seem to be the same thing to him. He wants to get his fingers on machinery.

I advise him not to be in any hurry about going back. The curious thing about it is that he can remember other and former lives of his on earth. Many out here have no more memory of their former lives, before the last one, than they had while in the body. This is not a place where everyone knows everything—far from it. Most souls are nearly as blind as they were in life.

The boy was an inventor in a prior incarnation, and he came out this time by an accident, he says. He should stay here a little longer, I think, to get a stronger rhythm for a return. That is only my idea. I am so interested in the boy that I should like to keep him, and perhaps that influences my judgment somewhat.

•

You see, we are still human.

You asked me some questions, did you not? Will you speak them aloud? I can hear.

Yes, I feel considerably younger than I have felt for a long time, and I am well. At first I felt about as I did in my illness, with times of depression and times of freedom from depression; but now I am all right. My body does not give me much trouble.

I believe that old people grow younger here until they reach their prime again, and that then they may hold that for a long time.

You see, I have not become all-wise. I have been able to pick up a good deal of knowledge which I had forgotten; but about all the details of this life I still have much to learn.

Your curiosity will help me to study conditions and to make inquiries, which otherwise I might not have made for a long time, if ever. Most people do not seem to learn much out here, except that naturally they learn the best and easiest way of getting on, as in earth life.

Yes, there are schools here where any who wish for instruction can receive it—if they are fit. But there are only a few *great* teachers. The average college professor is not a being of supreme wisdom, whether here or there.

L E T T E R

II

The Pattern World

There is something I want to qualify in what I said the other day, that there is nothing out here which has not existed on the earth. Since then I have learned that that statement is not exactly true. There are strata here. This I have learned recently. I still believe that in the lowest stratum next the earth all or nearly all that exists has existed on earth in dense matter. Go a little farther up, a little farther away—how far I cannot say by actual measurement; but the other night in exploring I got into the world of patterns, the paradigms—if that is the word—of things which *are to be* on earth. I saw forms of things which, so far as I know, have not existed on your planet — inventions, for example. I saw wings that man could adjust to himself. I saw also new forms of flying-machines. I saw model cities, and towers with strange winglike projections on them, of which I could not imagine the use. The progress of mechanical invention is evidently only begun.

•

Another time I will go on, farther up in that world of pattern forms, and see if I can learn what lies beyond it.

Bear this in mind: I merely tell you stories, as an earthly traveler would tell, of the things I see. Sometimes my interpretation of them may be wrong.

When I was in the place which we will call the pattern world, I saw almost nobody there—only an occasional lone voyager like myself. I naturally infer from this that but few of those who leave the earth go up there at all. I think from what I have seen, and from conversations I have had with men and women souls, that most of them do not get very far from the earth, even out here.

It is strange, but many persons seem to be in the regular orthodox heaven, singing in white robes, with crowns on their heads and with harps in their hands. There is a region which out-siders call "the heaven country."

There is also, they tell me, a fiery hell, with at least the smell of brimstone; but so far I have not been there. Some day when I feel strong I will look in, and if it is not too depressing I will go farther—if they will let me.

For the present I am looking about here and there, and I have not studied carefully any place as yet.

32

•

I took the boy, whose name by the way is Lionel, out with me yesterday. Perhaps we ought to say last night, for your day is our night when we are on your side of this great hollow sphere. You and the solid earth are in the center of our sphere.

I took the boy out with me for what you would call a walk.

First we went to the old quarter of Paris, where I used to live in a former life; but Lionel could not see anything, and when I pointed out certain buildings to him, he asked me quite sincerely if I were dreaming. I must have some faculty which is not generally developed among my fellow citizens in the astral country. So when the boy found that Paris was only a figment of my imagination—he used to live in Boston— I took him to see heaven. He remarked:

"Why, this must be the place my grandmother used to tell me about. But where is God?"

That I could not tell him; but, on looking again, we saw that nearly everybody was gazing in one direction. We also gazed with the others, and saw a great light, like a sun, only it was softer and less dazzling than the material sun.

"That," I said to the boy, "is what they see who see God."

And now I have something strange to tell you; for, as we gazed at that light, slowly there

33

took form between us and it the figure which we are accustomed to see represented as that of the Christ. He smiled at the people and stretched out His hands to them.

Then the scene changed, and He had on His left arm a lamb; and then again He stood as if transfigured upon a mountain; then He spoke and taught them. We could hear His voice. And then He vanished from our sight.

LETTER
12

FORMS REAL AND UNREAL

When I first came out here I was so interested in what I saw that I did not question much as to the manner of the seeing. But lately—especially since writing the last letter or two—I have begun to notice a difference between objects that at a superficial glance seem to be of much the same substance. For example, I can sometimes see a difference between those things which have existed on earth unquestionably, such as the forms of men and women, and other things which, while visualized and seemingly palpable, may be, and probably are, but thought-creations.

This idea came to me while looking on at the dramas of the heaven country, and it was forced upon me with greater power while making other and recent explorations in that which I have called the pattern world.

Later I may be able to distinguish at a glance between these two classes of seeming objects. For example, if I encounter here a being, or what

•

seems a being, and if I am told that it is some famous character in fiction, such as Jean Valjean in Hugo's *Les Misérables*, I shall have reason to believe that I have seen a thought-form of sufficient vitality to stand alone, as a quasi-entity in this world of tenuous matter. So far I have not encountered any such characters.

Of course, unless I were able to hold converse with a being, a form, or saw others do so, I could not positively state that it had an essential existence. Hereafter I shall often put things to the test in this way. If I can talk to a seeming entity, and if it can answer me, I am justified in considering it as a reality. A character in fiction, or any other mental creation, however vivid as a picture, would have no soul, no unit of force, no real self. Whatever comes to me merely as a picture I shall try to submit to this test.

If I see a peculiar form of tree or animal, and can touch and feel it—for the senses here are quite as acute as those of earth—I know that it exists in the subtle matter of this plane.

I believe that all the beings whom I have seen here are real; but if I can find one that is not—a being which I cannot feel when I touch it and which cannot respond to my questions— I shall have a datum for my hypothesis that thought-forms of beings, as well as things, may have sufficient cohesion to seem real.

It is undoubtedly true that there is no spirit without substance, no substance without spirit, latent or expressed; but a painting of a man may seem at a distance to be a man.

Can there exist deliberate thought-creations here, deliberate and purposive creations? I believe so. Such a thought-form would probably have to be very intense in order to persist.

It seems to me that I had better settle this question to my own satisfaction before talking any more about it.

LETTER
13

A FOLIO OF PARACELSUS

The other day I asked my Teacher to show me the archives in which those who had lived out here had recorded their observations, if such existed. He said:

"You were a great reader of books when you were on the earth. Come."

We entered a vast building like a library, and I caught my breath in wonder. It was not the architecture of the building which struck me, but the quantities of books and records. There must have been millions of them.

I asked the Teacher if all the books were here. He smiled and said:

"Are there not enough? You can make your choice."

I asked if the volumes were arranged by subjects.

"There is an arrangement," he answered. "What do you want?"

•

I said that I should like to see the books in which were written the accounts of explorations which other men had made in this (to me) still slightly known country.

He smiled again, and took from a shelf a thick volume. It was printed in large black type.

"Who wrote this book?" I asked.

"There is a signature," he replied.

I looked at the end and saw the signature: it was that used by Paracelsus.

"When did he write this?"

"Soon after he came out. It was written between his Paracelsus life and his next one on earth."

The book which I had opened was a treatise on spirits, human, angelic, and elemental. It began with the definition of a human spirit as a spirit which had had the experience of life in human form; and it defined an elemental spirit as a spirit of more or less developed self-consciousness which had not yet had that experience.

Then the author defined an angel as a spirit of a high order which had not had, and probably would not have in future, such experience in matter.

He went on to advise his readers that there was one way to determine whether a being of the subtler world was an angel or merely a

•

human or an elemental spirit, and that was by the greater brilliancy of the light which surrounded an angel.

I will perhaps say more on this subject another night. I must rest now.

LETTER
14

A Roman Toga

One thing which makes this country so interesting to me is its lack of conventionality. No two persons are dressed in the same way—or no, I do not mean that exactly, but many are so eccentrically dressed that their appearance gives variety to the whole.

My own clothes are, as a rule, similar to those I wore on earth, though I have as an experiment, when dwelling in thought on one of my long-past lives, put on the garments of the period.

It is easy to get the clothes one wants here. I do not know how I became possessed of the garments which I wore on coming out; but when I began to take notice of such things, I found myself dressed as usual. I am not yet sure whether I brought my clothes with me.

There are many people here in costumes of the ancient days. I do not infer from this fact that they have been here all those ages. I think they wear such clothes because they like them.

•

As a rule, most persons stay near the place where they lived on earth; but I have been a wanderer from the first. I go rapidly from one country to another. One night (or day with you) I may take my rest in America; the next night I may rest in Paris. I have spent hours of repose on the divan in your sitting room, and you did not know that I was there. I doubt, though, if I could stay for hours in your house when I was myself awake without your sensing my presence.

Do not think, however, from what I have just said, that it is necessary for me to rest on the solid matter of your world. Not at all. We can rest on the tenuous substance of our own world.

One day, when I had been here only a short time, I saw a woman dressed in a Greek costume, and asked her where she got her clothes. She replied that she had made them. I asked her how, and she said:

"Why, first I made a pattern in my mind, and then the thing became a garment."

"Did you take every stitch?"

"Not as I should have done on earth."

I looked closer and saw that the whole garment seemed to be in one piece, and that it was caught on the shoulders by jeweled pins. I asked where she got the jeweled pins, and she said that a friend had given them to her. Then I asked where the friend had got them. She told me that she did not know, but that she would ask him. Soon after that she left me, and I have not seen her since, so the question is still unanswered.

I began an experiment to see if I also could make things. It was then that I conceived the idea of wearing a Roman toga, but for the life of me I could not remember what a Roman toga looked like.

When next I met the Teacher, I told him of my wish to wear a toga of my own making, and he carefully showed me how to create garments such as I desired: To fix the pattern and shape clearly in my mind, to visualize it, and then by power of desire to draw the subtle matter of the thought-world round the pattern, so as actually to form the garment.

"Then," I said, "the matter of the thought-world, as you call it, is not the same kind of matter as that of my body, for instance?"

"In the last analysis," he answered, "there is only one kind of matter in both worlds; but there is a great difference in vibration and tenuity."

Now the thought-substance of which our garments are formed seems to be an extremely tenuous form of matter, while our bodies seem to be pretty solid. We do not feel at all like transparent angels sitting on damp clouds. Were it not for the quickness with which I get over space, I should think sometimes that my body was as solid as ever.

I can often see you, and to me *you* seem tenuous. It is all, I suppose, the old question of adjusting to environment. At first I could not do it, and had some trouble in learning to adjust the amount of energy necessary for each particular action. So little energy is required here to move myself about that at first when I started to go a short distance—say, a few yards—I would find myself a mile away. But I am now pretty well adjusted.

I must be storing up energy here for a good hard life when I return to the earth again. The hardest work I do now is to come and write through your hand, but you offer less and less resistance as time goes on. In the beginning it took all my strength; now it takes only a comparatively small effort. Yet I could not do it long at a time without using your own vitality, and that I will not do.

You may have noticed that you are no longer fatigued after the writing, though you used to be at first.

But I was speaking of the lack of conventionality out here. Souls hail each other when they want to, without much ceremony. I have seen a few old women who were afraid to talk to a stranger, but probably they had not been here long and the earth habits still clung to them.

Do not think, however, that society here is too free and easy. It is not that, but men and women do not seem to be so afraid of each other as they were on earth.

L E T T E R
15

A Thing to Be Forgotten

I want to say a word to those who are about to die. I want to beg them to forget their bodies as soon as possible after the change which they call death.

Oh, the terrible curiosity to go back and look upon that *thing* which we once believed to be ourselves! The thought comes to us now and then so powerfully that it acts in a way against our will and draws us back to *it*. With some it is a morbid obsession, and many cannot get free from it while there remains a shred of flesh on the bones which they once leaned upon.

Tell them to forget it altogether, to force the thought away, to go out into the other life free. Looking back upon the past is sometimes good, but not upon this relic of the past.

It is so easy to look into the coffin, because the body which we wear now is itself a light in a dark place, and it can penetrate grosser matter. I have been back myself a few times, but am determined to go back no more. Yet some day the thought may come to me again with compelling insistence to see how *it* is getting on.

I do not want to shock or pain you—only to warn you. It is sad to see the sight which inevitably meets one in the grave. That may be the reason why many souls who have not been here long are so melancholy. They return again and again to the place which they should not visit.

You know that out here if we think intently of a place, we are apt to find ourselves there. The body which we use is so light that it can follow thought almost without effort. Tell them not to do it.

47

One day while walking down an avenue of trees—for we have trees here—I met a tall woman in a long black garment. She was weeping—for we have tears here also. I asked her why she wept, and she turned to me eyes of unutterable sadness.

"I have been back to *it*," she said.

My heart ached for her, because I knew how she felt. The shock of the first visit is repeated each time, as the thing one sees is less and less what we like to think of ourselves as being.

Often I remember that tall woman in black, walking down the avenue of trees and weeping. It is partly curiosity that draws one back, partly magnetic attraction; but it can do no good. It is better to forget it.

I have sometimes longed, from sheer scientific interest, to ask my boy Lionel if he had been back to his body; but I have not asked him for fear of putting the idea into his mind. He has such a restless curiosity. Perhaps those who go out as children have less of that morbid instinct than we have.

If we could only remember in life that the form which we call ourself is not our real immortal self at all, we would not give it such an exaggerated importance, though we would nevertheless take needful care of it.

48

As a rule, those who say that they have been long here do not seem old. I asked the Teacher why, and he said that after a time an old person forgets that he is old, that the tendency is to grow young in thought and therefore young in appearance, that the body tends to take the form which we hold of it in our minds, that the law of rhythm works here as elsewhere.

Children grow up out here, and they may even go on to a sort of old age if that is the expectation of the mind; but the tendency is to keep the prime, to go forward or back towards the best period, and then to hold that until the irresistible attraction of the earth asserts itself again.

•

A Thing to Be Forgotten

Most of the men and women here do not
know that they have lived many times in flesh.
They remember their latest life more or less
vividly, but all before that seems like a dream.
One should always keep the memory of the past
as clear as possible. It helps one to construct
the future.

Those people who think of their departed
friends as being all-wise, how disappointed they
would be if they could know that the life on this
side is only an extension of the life on earth! If
the thoughts and desires there have been only
for material pleasures, the thoughts and desires
here are likely to be the same. I have met veritable saints since coming out; but they have
been men and women who held in earth life the
saintly ideal, and who now are free to live it.

Life can be so free here! There is none of that
machinery of living which makes people on
earth such slaves. In our world a man is held
only by his thoughts. If they are free, he is free.

Few, though, are of my philosophic spirit.
There are more saints here than philosophers,
as the highest ideal of most persons, when intensely active, has been towards the religious
rather than the philosophic life.

I think the happiest people I have met on
this side have been the painters. Our matter is so
light and subtle, and so easily handled, that it

49

falls readily into the forms of the imagination. There are beautiful pictures here. Some of our artists try to impress their pictures upon the mental eyes of the artists of earth, and they often succeed in doing so.

There is joy in the heart of one of our real artists when a fellow craftsman on your side catches an idea from him and puts it into execution. He may not always be able to see clearly how well the second man works out the idea, for it requires a special gift or a special training to *see* from one form of matter into the other; but the inspiring spirit catches the thought in the inspired one's mind, and knows that a conception of his own is being executed upon the earth.

With poets it is the same. There are lovely lyrics composed out here and impressed upon the receptive minds of earthly poets. A poet told me that it was easier to do that with a short lyric than with an epic or a drama, where a long-continued effort was necessary.

It is much the same with musicians. Whenever you go to a concert where beautiful music is being played, there is probably all round you a crowd of music-loving spirits, drinking in the harmonies. Music on earth is much enjoyed on this side. It can be heard. But no sensitive spirit likes to go near a place where bad strumming is going on. We prefer the music of stringed instruments. Of all earthly things, sound reaches most directly into this plane of life. Tell that to the musicians.

If they could only hear our music! I did not understand music on earth, but now my ears are becoming adjusted. It seems sometimes as if you must hear our music over there, as we hear yours.

You may have wondered how I spend my time and where I go. There is a lovely spot in the country which I never tire of visiting. It is on the side of a mountain, not far from my own city. There is a little road winding round a hill, and just above the road is a hut, a roofed enclosure with the lower side open. Sometimes I stay there for hours and listen to the rippling of the brook which runs beside the road. The tall slender trees have become like brothers to me. At first I cannot see the material trees very clearly; but I go into the little hut which is made of fresh clean boards with a sweet smell, and I lie down on the shelf or bunk along the wall; then I close my eyes and by an effort—or no, it is not what I would call an effort, but by a sort of drifting—I can see the beautiful place. But you must know that this is in the nighttime there, and I see it by the light of myself. That is why we travel in the dark part of the twenty-four hours, for in the bright sunlight we cannot see at all. Our light is put out by the cruder light of the sun.

One night I took the boy Lionel there with me, leaving him in the hut while I went a little distance away. Looking back, I saw the whole hut illuminated by a lovely radiance—the radiance of Lionel himself. The little building, which has a peaked roof, looked like a pearl lighted from within. It was a beautiful experience.

I then went to Lionel and told him to go in his turn a little distance away, while I took his place in the hut. I was curious to know if he would see the same phenomenon when I lay there, if I could shed such a light through dense matter—the boards of the building. When I called him to me afterwards and asked if he had seen anything strange, he said:

"What a wonderful man you are, Father! How did you make that hut seem to be on fire?"

Then I knew that he had seen the same thing I had seen.

But I am tired now and can write no more. Good night, and may you have pleasant dreams.

LETTER
16

THE SECOND WIFE OVER THERE

I am often called upon here to decide matters for others. Many people call me simply "the Judge"; but we bear, as a rule, the name that we last bore on earth.

Men and women come to me to settle all sorts of questions for them, questions of ethics, questions of expediency, even quarrels. Did you suppose that no one quarreled here? Many do. There are even long-standing feuds among them.

The holders of different opinions on religion are often hot in their arguments. Coming here with the same beliefs they had on earth, and being able to visualize their ideals and actually to experience the things they are expecting, two men who hold opposite creeds forcibly are each more intolerant than ever before. Each is certain that he is right and that the other is wrong. This stubbornness of belief is strongest with those who have been here only a short time. After a while they fall into a larger tolerance, living their own lives more and more, and enjoying the world of proofs and realizations which each soul builds for itself.

But I want to give you an illustration of the sort of questions on which I am asked to pass judgment.

There are two women here who in life were both married to one man, though not at the same time. The first woman died, then the man married again, and soon—not more than a year or two later—the man and his second wife both came out. The first wife considers herself the man's only wife, and she follows him about everywhere. She says that he promised to meet her in heaven. He is more inclined to the second wife, though he still feels affection for Wife No. 1. He is rather impatient at what he calls her unreasonableness. He told me one day that he would gladly give them both up, if he could be left in peace to carry out certain studies in which he is interested. These were among the people I met soon after I began to be strong myself here—it was not so very long ago; and the man has sought my society so much that the women, in order to be near him, have come along too.

One day they all three came to me and propounded their question—or, rather, Wife No. 1 propounded it. She said:

•

"This man is my husband. Should not, therefore, this other woman go far away and leave
him altogether with me?"

I asked Wife No. 2 what she had to say. Her
answer was that she would be all alone here
but for her husband, and that as she had had
him last, he now belonged more to her than to
the other.

In a flash the memory came to me of those
Sadducees who propounded a similar question
to Christ, and I quoted His answer as nearly as I
could remember it: that "when they shall rise
from the dead, they neither marry, nor are given
in marriage; but are as the angels which are
in heaven."

My answer was as much a staggerer for them
as their question had been for me, and they went
away to think about it.

When they were gone, I began myself to
ponder the question. I had already observed
that, whether or not all here are as the angels in
heaven, there does seem to be a good deal of
mating and rejoining of former mates. The sex
distinction is as real here as on the earth, though,
of course, its expression is not exactly the same.
I asked myself a good many questions which
perhaps would never have occurred to me but
for the troubles of this interesting triad, and I
thought of the man I had somewhere read about,

55

who said that he never knew his own opinion of anything until he tried to express it to somebody.

After a while the three came to me again and said that they had been talking things over, perhaps after the manner of angels in heaven; for Wife No. 1 told me that she had decided to "let" her husband spend a part of his time with the other woman, if he wanted to.

Now, the man had a sweetheart, a girl sweetheart, before he had either of his wives. The girl is out here somewhere, and the man often has a strong desire to try to find her. What opportunity he will now have to do so, I cannot say. The situation is rather depressing for the poor fellow. It is bad enough to have one person who insists on every minute of your society, without having two. And I think his case is not unusual. Perhaps the only way in which he can get free from his two insistent companions is by going back to the earth.

There is a way, however, by which he could secure solitude; but he does not know of it. A man who knows how can isolate himself here as well as he could on earth; he can build round himself a wall which only the eyes of a great initiate can pierce. I have not told this secret to my friend; but perhaps I shall some day, if it seems necessary for his development that he have a little solitude. At present it seems to me that he will learn more from adjusting to this double claim and trying to find the truth that lies in it. Perhaps he may learn that really, essentially, fundamentally, he does not "belong" to either of these women. The souls out here seem to belong to themselves, and after the first few years they get to love liberty so much that they are ready to yield a little of their claim upon others.

This is a great place in which to grow, if one really wants to grow; though few persons take advantage of its possibilities. Most are content to assimilate the experiences they had on earth. It would be depressing to one who did not realize that will is free, to see how souls let slip their opportunities here, even as they did on the moon-guarded planet.

There are teachers here who stand ready to help anyone who wishes their help in making real and deep studies in the mysteries of life—the life here, the life there, and in the remote past.

If a man understands that his recent sojourn on earth was merely the latest of a long series of lives, and if he concentrates his mind towards recovering the memories of the distant past, he can recover them. Some persons may think that the mere dropping of the veil of matter should free the soul from all obscuration; but, as on earth so out here, "things are not thus and so because they ought to be, but because they are."

We draw to ourselves the experiences which we are ready for and which we demand, and most souls do not demand enough here, any more than they did in life. Tell them to demand more, and the demand will be answered.

•

L E T T E R

17

INDIVIDUAL HELLS

Some time ago I told you of my intention to visit hell; but when I began investigations on that line there proved to be many hells.

Each man who is not content with the orthodox hell of fire and brimstone builds one out of mind-stuff suited to his imaginative need.

I believe that men place themselves in hell, that no God puts them there. I began looking for a hell of fire and brimstone, and found it. Dante must have seen the same things I saw.

But there are other and individual hells ——

(The writing suddenly stopped, for no apparent reason, and was not continued that night.—EB)

•

L E T T E R
18

A LITTLE HOME IN HEAVEN

I have met a very interesting man since last I wrote to you. He is a lover who for ten years waited here for his love to come to him.

They said on earth that he was dead, and they urged her to love another; but she could not forget him, for every night he met her soul in dreams, every night she came out to him here, and sometimes she could recall on waking all that he had said to her in sleep. She had told him that she would not delay long in the sunshine world, but would come out to him in the self-lighted world.

Only a little while ago she came. He had been long getting ready for her coming, and had built in the substance of this world the little home he had planned to build for her in the outer world.

He told me how one night when she came to him in dream, she said that she would rejoin him on the morrow, never to leave him again. He was startled, and would almost have stayed her; because he had died a sudden and painful death, and he dreaded pain for her. Always he had watched over her, warning her of danger; but this time he felt, after the first shock of the message was over, that she was really coming. And he was very happy.

He had found no other love out here; for when one leaves the earth full of a great affection, and when the earthly loved one does not forget, the tie can hold for many years unweakened. You on the earth have forgotten so much of what you learned here that you do not realize how your thought of us can make us happy, do not realize how your forgetfulness of us can throw us back entirely upon ourselves.

61

Often those who go farthest here, who really grow in spirituality, are those whose loves have forgotten them on earth; but it is sad to be forgotten, nevertheless.

It is a bitter power you make possible to us when you thus throw us back upon ourselves; and not all souls are strong enough or aspiring enough to make use of the lonely impetus that might help them to scale the ladder of spiritual knowledge.

But to return to my lovers. All that day he remained near her. He would not rest; for, as I have told you, we generally rest a little when the sun shines on the earth. All that day he remained near her. He could not see her body, for the rays of sunlight were too strong for him. But, after hours of waiting, suddenly he felt a hand in his, and though she was invisible to him, yet he knew that she was *here*. And he spoke to her, using such words as he would have used on earth. She did not seem to understand. He spoke again, and still she did not answer; but he knew from the pressure of her hand that she realized his presence. So hand in hand they stood there in the darkness of the sunlight, the man able to speak because of his long experience in this world of subtle sounds, the woman speechless and bewildered, but still clinging to his hand.

62

When the sunshine went away, he was able to see her face, and her eyes were wide and frightened; but still she seemed held to the room in which lay the body which had been she. It was summer, and the windows were open. He sought to draw her away into the perfumed night which to them was day; but she held his hand and would not let him go.

As last he drew her away a short distance and spoke to her again. Now she heard and answered him.

"Beloved," she said, "which is I? For I see myself—I feel myself—back there also. I seem to be in two places. Which I is really I?"

●

He comforted her with loving words. He was still afraid to caress her, for the touch of souls is very keen, and he feared lest she should go back into the form which seemed to be so near them, and thus be lost to him again. But though she had often come to him in dreams, it had not been so vividly as this time, and he felt that she had really passed through the great change.

She still clung to his hand, yet seemed afraid to go out with him—out and away from *it*. He stayed there with her all that night and all the next day, when the darkening sun came again, and again he could not see her.

Once the well-meaning friends of his beloved disturbed her body, doing those sacred offices which seem so necessary to the living, but which may sorely disturb the dead.

He stayed with her the second night and all the second day. He could hear the sobs of her grieving parents, though they could not see either him or their daughter; but on the second night the little dog of his love came into the room where *it* lay, the room in which their two souls still stood, and the little dog saw them and whined piteously. The man could hear it, and she also could hear it.

And now she could hear him more plainly when he spoke to her.

"Where will they take *it*?" she asked him.

He recalled the time when he had been held spellbound near his own lifeless form, over which his loved one had shed bitter tears. And he asked her if it would not be better to come away altogether; but she could not, or thought she could not.

On the third day he knew from the agitation of his love that they were placing her body in the coffin. After a while he felt, though he could not see, that many other persons were in the room, and he heard mournful music. Music can reach from one world to another, can be heard far more plainly than human voices, which generally cannot be heard at all except by the trained listener.

By and by his love was sorely agitated, and he also, through sympathy with her; and they felt themselves going slowly—oh, so slowly!—along. And he said to her:

"Do not be grieved. They are taking *it* to the burial; but you are safe with me." He knew that she was much troubled.

It is not for nothing that over the house of death there always hangs a strange hush, not to be explained by the mere losing of the loved one. Those who remain behind feel, though they cannot see, the soul of the one who has gone out. Their souls are full of sympathy for him in his bewilderment.

•

The change need not be painful if one would only remember that it has been passed through before; but one so easily forgets. We sometimes call the earth the Valley of Forgetfulness.

During the days and weeks that followed, this lover remained with his loved one, ever trying to draw her away from the earth and from *it*, which had for her, as for so many, a fearsome fascination.

It is said that the souls of those who have lived long on earth more easily detach themselves; but this woman was still young, only about thirty, and even with the help of her lover it was a little time before she could get free.

But one day (or night, as you would say) he showed her the home which he had built for her, and it was literally a mansion in the sky. She entered with him, and it became their home.

Sometimes he leaves her for a little while, or she leaves him; for the joy of being together is heightened here, as on the earth, by an occasional separation; but not until she was content and accustomed to the new life did he leave her at all.

During the first days the habit of earthly hunger often held her, and he tried to appease it by giving her the softer substance which we know here. Gradually she became weaned altogether from the earth and the habits of the earth, only going back occasionally in a dream to her father and mother.

Do not disregard your dreams about the dead. They always mean something. They do not always mean what the dream would seem to signify; for the door between the two worlds is very narrow, and thoughts are often shaken out of place in passing through. But dreams about the dead mean something. We can reach you in that way.

I came to you in a dream the other night, standing behind and outside the gate of a walled garden in which you were enclosed. I smiled and beckoned you to come out to stay. I only meant that you should come out in spirit; for if you come out occasionally, it is easier for me to go into your world.

Good night.

LETTER
19

THE MAN WHO FOUND GOD

There seems to be no way in which I can better teach you about this life, so strange to you, than by telling my experiences and conversations with men and women here.

I said one night not long ago that I had met more saints than philosophers, and I want to tell you now about a man who seems to be a genuine saint. Yes, there are little saints and great saints, as there are little sinners and great sinners.

One day I was walking on a mountaintop. I say "walking," for it seemed about the same, though it takes but little energy to walk here.

On the mountaintop I saw a man standing alone. He was looking out and far away, but I could not see what he was looking at. He was abstracted and communing with himself, or with some presence of which I was unaware.

I waited for some time. At last, drawing a long breath—for we breathe here—he turned his eyes to me and said, with a kind smile:

•

"Can I do anything for you, brother?"

I was embarrassed for a moment, feeling that I might have intruded upon some sweet communion.

"If I am not too bold in asking," I said, "would you tell me what you were thinking as you stood there looking into space?"

I was conscious of my presumption; but being so determined to learn what can be known, if sometimes I am too bold in making inquiries, I feel that my very earnestness may win for me the forgiveness of those I question.

This man had a beautiful beardless face and young-looking eyes; but his garments were the ordinary garments of one who thinks little or nothing of his appearance. That very unconsciousness of the outer form may sometimes give it a peculiar majesty.

He looked at me in silence for a moment; then he said:

"I was trying to draw near to God."

"And what is God?" I asked; "and where is God?"

He smiled. I never saw a smile like his, as he answered:

"God is everywhere. God *is*."

"What is He?" I persisted; and again he repeated, but with a different emphasis:

"*God* is."

●

"What do you mean?" I asked.

"God *is*, *God* is," he said.

I do not know how his meaning was conveyed to me, perhaps by sympathy; but it suddenly flashed into my mind that when he said, "God *is*," he expressed the completest realization of God which is possible to the spirit; and when he said, "*God* is," he meant me to understand that there was no being, nothing that is, except God.

There must have been in my face a reflection of what I felt, for the saint then said to me:

"Do you not also know that He *is*, and that all that is, is He?"

"I am beginning to feel what you mean," I answered, "though I doubtless feel but a little of it."

He smiled, and made no reply; but my mind was full of questions.

"When you were on earth," I said, "did you think much about God?"

"Always. I thought of little else. I sought Him everywhere, but seemed only at times to get flashes of consciousness as to what He really was. Sometimes when praying, for I prayed much, there would come to me suddenly the question, 'To what are you praying?' And I would answer aloud, 'To God, to God!' But though I prayed to Him every day for years, only occasionally did I get a flash of that true consciousness of God. Finally, one day when I was alone in the woods, there came the great revelation. It came not in any form of words, but rather in a wordless and formless wonder, too vast for the limitation of thought. I fell upon the ground and must have lost consciousness, for after a while—how long a time I do not know—I awoke, and got up and looked about me. Then gradually I remembered the experience which had been too big for me while I was feeling it.

"I could put into the form of words the realization which had been too much for my mortality to bear, and the words I used to myself were, 'All that is, is God.' It seemed very simple, yet it was far from simple. 'All that is, is God.' That must include me and all my fellow beings, human and animal; even the trees and the birds and the rivers must be a part of God, if God were all that is.

"From that moment life assumed a new meaning for me. I could not see a human face without remembering the revelation—that the human being I saw was a part of God. When my dog looked at me, I said to him aloud, 'You are a part of God.' When I stood beside a river and listened to the sound of its waters, I said to myself, 'I am listening to the voice of God.' When a fellow being was angry with me, I asked myself, 'In what way have I offended God?'

When one spoke lovingly to me, I said, 'God is loving me now,' and the realization nearly took my breath away. Life became unbelievably beautiful.

"Theretofore I had been so absorbed in God, in trying to find God, that I had not given much thought to my fellow beings, and had even neglected those nearest me; but from that day I began to mingle with my human brethren. I found that as more and more I sought God in them, more and more God responded to me through them. And life became still more wonderful.

"Sometimes I tried to tell others what I felt, but they did not always understand me. It was thus I began to realize that God had purposely, for some reason of His own, covered Himself in veils. Was it that He might have the pleasure of tearing them away? If so, I would help Him all I could. So I tried to make other men grasp the knowledge for God which I myself had attained. For years I taught men. At first I wanted to teach everybody; but I soon came to see that that was impossible, and so I selected a few who called themselves my disciples. They did not always tell the world that they were my disciples, because I asked them not to do so. But I urged each of them to give to someone as much as possible of the knowledge that I had given to him. And so I think that many have come to feel a little of the wonder which was revealed to me that day alone in the woods, when I awoke to the knowledge that God *is, God* is."

Then the saint turned and left me, with all my questions unanswered. I wanted to ask him when and how he had left the earth, and what work he was doing out here—but he was gone!

Perhaps I shall see him again some day. But whether I do or not, he has given me something which I in turn give to you, as he himself desired to give it to the world.

That is all for tonight.

L E T T E R
20

THE LEISURE OF THE SOUL

One of the joys of being here is the leisure for dreaming and for getting acquainted with oneself.

Of course there is plenty to do; but though I intend to go back to the world in a few years, I feel that there is time to get acquainted with myself. I tried to do that on earth, more or less; but here there are fewer demands on me. The mere labor of dressing and undressing is lighter, and I do not have to earn my living now, nor anybody else's.

You, too, could take time to loaf, if you thought you could. You can do practically anything you think you can do.

I propose, for instance, in a few years not only to pick up a general knowledge of the conditions of this four-dimensional world, but to go back over my other lives and assimilate what I learned in them. I want to make a synthesis of the complete experiences of my ego up to this

•

date, and to judge from that synthesis what I can do in the future with least resistance. I believe, but am not quite sure, that I can bring back much of this knowledge with me when I am born again.

I shall try to tell you—or some of you—when and about where to look for me again. Oh, don't be startled! It will not be for some time yet. An early date would necessitate hurry, and I do not wish to hurry. I could probably force the coming back, but that would be unwise, for I should then come back with less power than I want. Action and reaction being opposite and equal, and the unit, or ego, being able to generate only *so much* energy in a given time, it is better for me to rest in this condition of light matter until I have accumulated energy enough to come back with power. I shall not do, however, as many souls do; they stay out here until they are as tired of this world as they formerly were tired of the earth, and then are driven back half unconsciously by the irresistible force of the tide of rhythm. I want to guide that rhythm.

Since I have been here, one man whom I know has gone back to the earth. He was about ready to go when I first found him. The strange part of it was that he himself did not understand his condition. He complained of being tired of things and of wanting to rest much. That was probably a natural instinct for rest, in preparation for the supreme effort of opening the doors of matter again. It is easy to come out here, but it requires some effort to go *from* this world into yours.

I know where that soul is now, for the Teacher told me. I had spoken to the Teacher about him, but he already knew of his existence. It was rather strange, for the man was one in whom I should have fancied that the Teacher would have taken little interest. But one never knows. Perhaps in his next life he may really begin to study the philosophy which *they* teach.

But I was speaking of the larger leisure out here. I wish you could arrange your life so as to have a little more leisure. I do not want you to be lazy, but the passive conditions of the mind are quite as valuable as the active conditions. It is when you are passive that we can reach you. When your mind and body are always occupied, it is difficult to impress you with any message of the soul. Find a little more time each day for doing nothing at all. It is good to do nothing sometimes; then the semiconscious parts of your mind can work. They can remind you that there is an inner life: for the inner life that is "capable" to you on earth is really the point of contact with the world in which we live.

I have said that the two worlds touch, and they touch through the inner. You go in to come

75

out. It is a paradox, and paradoxes conceal great truths. Contradictions are not truths, but a paradox is not a contradiction.

There is a great difference in the length of time that people stay out here. You talk of being homesick. There are souls here who are homesick for the earth. They sometimes go back almost at once, which is generally a mistake. Unless one is young and still has a store of unused energy saved over from the last life, in going back to the earth too soon one lacks the force of a strong rebound.

It is strange to see a man here as homesick for the earth as certain poets and dreamers on earth are homesick for the inner life.

This use of the terms "outer" and "inner" may seem confusing; but you must remember that while you go *in* to come to us, we go *out* to come to you. In our normal state here we are living almost a subjective life. We become more and more objective as we touch your world. You become more and more subjective as you touch our world. If you only knew it, you could come to us at almost any time for a brief visit—I mean, by going deep enough into yourself.

If you want to try the experiment and will not be afraid, I can take you out here without your quite losing consciousness in your body— I mean without your being in deep sleep. You can call me when you want to make a trial. If I do not come at once, do not be discouraged. Of course at the moment I might be doing something else; but in that case I will come at another time.

There is no hurry. That is what I want to impress upon you. What you do not do this year you can perhaps do next year; but if you are always rushing after things, you can accomplish little in this particular work. Eternity is long enough for the full development of the ego of man. Eternity seems to have been designed for that end. That was a sound statement which was given at one time: "The object of life is life." I have realized that more fully since I had an opportunity to study eternity from a new angle. This is a very good angle from which to view both time and eternity. I see now what I did not see before, that I myself have never wasted any time. Even my failures were a valuable part of my experience. We lose to gain again. We go in and out of power sometimes as we go in and out of life, to learn what is there and outside. In this as in all things, the object of life is life.

Do not hurry. A man may grow gradually into power and knowledge, or he may take them by force. Will is free. But the gradual growth has a less powerful reaction.

•

L E T T E R
21

THE SERPENT OF ETERNITY

I want to talk to you tonight about eternity. Until I came out, I never had a grasp on that problem. I thought only in terms of months and years and centuries; now I see the full sweep of the circle. The comings out and the goings into matter are no more than the systole and the diastole of the ego-heart; and, speaking from the standpoint of eternity, they are relatively as brief. To you a lifetime is a long time. It used to seem so to me, but it does not seem so now.

People are always saying, "If I had my life to live over, I would do so and so." Now, no man has any particular life to live over, any more than the heart can go back and beat over again the beat of the second previous; but every man has his next life to prepare for. Suppose you have made a botch of your existence. Most men have, viewed from the standpoint of their highest ideal; but every man who can think must have assimilated some experience which he can carry over

•

with him. He may not, on coming out into the sunlight of another life on earth, be able to remember the details of his former experience, though some men can recall them by a sufficient training and a fixed will; but the tendencies of any given life, the unexplained impulses and desires, are in nearly all cases brought over.

You should get away from the mental habit of regarding your present life as the only one, get rid of the idea that the life you expect to lead on this side, after your death, is to be an endless existence in one state. You could no more endure such an endless existence in the subtle matter of the inner world than you could endure to live forever in the gross matter in which you are now encased. You would weary of it. You could not support it.

Do get this idea of rhythm into your brain. All beings are subject to the law of rhythm, even the gods—though in a greater way than ourselves, with longer periods of flux and reflux.

I did not want to leave the earth; I fought against it until the last; but now I see that my coming out was inevitable because of the conditions. Had I begun earlier I might have provisioned my craft for a longer cruise; but when the coal and water had run out, I had to make port.

It is possible to provision even a small life-craft for a longer voyage than the allotted three-

•

score years and ten; but one must economize the coal and not waste the water. There are some who will understand that water is the fluid of life.

Many persons resent the idea that the life after death is not eternal, a never-ending progression in spiritual realms; though few who so object have much of an idea what they mean when they talk of spiritual realms.

Life everlasting is possible to all souls—yes; but it is not possible to go on forever in one direction. Evolution is a curve. Eternity is a circle, a serpent that swallows its own tail. Until you are willing to go in and out of dense matter, you will never learn to transcend matter. There are those who can stay in or out at will and, relatively speaking, as long as they choose; but they are never those who shrink from either form of life.

I used to shrink from what I called death. There are those on this side who shrink from what *they* call death. Do you know what they call death? It is rebirth into the world. Yes, even so.

There are many here who are as ignorant of rhythm as most people on your side. I have met men and women who did not even know that they would go back to the earth again, who talked of the "great change" as the men of earth talk of dying, and of all that lay beyond as "unproved and unprovable." It would be tragic if it were not so absurd.

When I knew that I had to die, I determined to carry with me memory, philosophy, and reason.

Now I want to say something which will perhaps surprise you. There is a man who wrote a book called *The Law of Psychic Phenomena*, and in that book he said certain things of those two parts of the mind which he called the subjective and the objective. He said that the subjective mind was incapable of inductive reasoning, that the subjective mind would accept any premise given it by the objective mind, and would reason from that premise with matchless logic; but that it could not go behind the premise, that it could not reason backwards.

Now, remember that in this form of matter where I am men are living principally a subjective life, as men on earth live principally an objective life. These people here, being in the subjective, reason from the premises already given them during their objective or earth existence. That is why most of those who last lived in the so-called Western lands, where the idea of rhythm or rebirth is unpopular, came out here with the fixed idea that they would not go back into earth life. Hence most of them still reason from that premise.

•

Do you not understand that what you believe you are going to be out here is largely determinative of what you will be? Those who do not believe in rebirth cannot forever escape the rhythm of rebirth; but they hold to their belief until the tide of rhythm sweeps them along with it and forces them into gross matter again, into which they go quite unprepared, carrying with them almost no memory of their life out here. They carried out here the memory of the earth life because they expected so to carry it.

Many Orientals who have always believed in rebirth remember their former lives, because they expected to remember them.

Yes, when I realized that I had to leave the earth, I laid a spell upon myself. I determined to remember through both the going out and the subsequent coming in. Of course I cannot swear now to remember everything when I come into heavy matter again; but I am determined to do so if possible; and I shall succeed to some extent if I do not get the wrong mother. I intend to take great care on that point, and to choose a mother who is familiar with the idea of rebirth. If possible, I want to choose a mother who actually knew me in my last life as ——, and who, if I shall announce in childhood that I am that same —— whom she knew when a young girl, will not chide me and drive me back into myself with her doubts.

I believe that many children carry over into earth life memories of their lives out here, but that those memories are afterwards lost by reason of the suggestion constantly given to children that they are newly created, "fresh from the hand of God," etc., etc.

Eternity is indeed long, and there are more things in earth and heaven than are dreamed of in the philosophy of the average teacher of children.

If you could only get hold of the idea of immortal life and *cling to it!* If you could realize yourself as being without beginning and without end, then you might commence to do things worthwhile. It is a wonderful consciousness, that consciousness of eternity. Small troubles seem indeed small to him who thinks of himself in the terms of a million years. You may make the figure a billion, or whatever you like, but the idea is the same. No man can grasp the idea of a million years, or a million dollars, or a million of anything; the figure is merely a symbol for a great quantity, whether it be years or gold pieces. The idea cannot be fixed; there will always be something that escapes. No millionaire knows exactly what he is worth at any given time; for there is always interest to be counted, and the

83

value is a shifting one. It is so with immortality.
Do not think of yourself as having lived a million
years, or a trillion years, but as truly immortal,
without beginning or end. The man who knows
himself to be rich is richer than the man who
says that he has a certain amount of money,
be the amount large or small. So rest in the
consciousness of eternity, and work in the consciousness of eternity.

That is all for tonight.

LETTER
22

A Brief for the Defendant

Tell the friend who is so anxious lest I do you harm by writing with your hand that the matter was thoroughly threshed out on this side between the Teacher and me before it began to take form on your side.

Ordinary mediumship, where the organism of a more or less unhealthy person on earth is opened indiscriminately for the entrance and obsession of any passing spirit, friendly or otherwise, is a very different proposition from this. Here I, who was your friend in the world, having passed beyond, reach back to instruct you from my greater knowledge on this side.

I am not making any opening in your nervous system through which irresponsible forces can enter and take possession of you. In fact, if any spirit, amiable or harmful, should make such an attempt, he would have to reckon with me, and I am not powerless. I know now, have both remembered and been taught, secrets by which I can protect you from what is generally known as mediumship. Furthermore, I advise you never, even at the urgent prayer of those whose loved ones have gone out—*never* to lend yourself to them. The wanderers in the so-called invisible world have no right to come and demand entrance through your organism, merely because it is so constituted that they could enter, any more than a street crowd would have the right to force its way into your home, merely because its members were curious, hungry, or cold. Do not allow it. Permission was once given, yes; but the case was exceptional and was not based on the personal desire or curiosity of anybody—not even yourself. I doubt if permission will ever be granted again.

Many things have changed since I began to write with you. At first I used your hand and arm from the outside—sometimes, as you remember, with such force as to make them lame the next day. Then, grown more familiar with the means at my disposal, I tried another method, and you noticed a change in the character of the writing. It began clumsily, with large and badly formed characters, gradually becoming clearer as my control of the instrument I was using was better established.

Now, for the last few times I have used still another and a third method. I enter your mind,

•

putting myself in absolute telepathic rapport with your mind, impressing upon your mind itself the things I wish to say. In order to write in this way, you have to make yourself utterly passive, stilling all individual thought and yielding yourself to my thought; but that is no more than you do every day in reading a fascinating book. You can give your mind to the author who leads you along, rapt and passive, by means of the printed page.

These experiments in perfecting a way of communication have been very interesting to me.

Tell your friend that I am not a child, nor a reckless experimentalist. Not only in my last life on earth but in many former lives I have been a student of the higher science, giving myself absolutely to truth and to the quest of truth. I have never wantonly used any human being to his or her detriment, and I certainly shall not begin with you, my true friend and student.

Nor shall I interfere in any way with your life, or with your studies and work. The idea is nonsensical. While I walked the world on two feet I was never considered a dangerous man. I have not changed my character merely by changing my clothes and putting on a lighter suit.

I have certain things to say to the world. At present you are the only person who can act as amanuensis for me. This is neither my fault nor yours. The question before us is not whether I want the letters written, or even whether you want to write them, but whether they will be beneficial to the world. I think they will. You think they may be. B—— thinks that they are not only immensely valuable, but unique. So-and-so and So-and-so have doubts and fears. I cannot help that, nor can you.

Bless their hearts! Why should they be so anxious to bolt the doors behind me? I shall certainly not try to run their affairs for them from this side. They are equal to their job, or they would not be able to hold it. But this is quite a different job which I have given myself, and you have kindly consented to help me.

You may not get much reward for your labor, save the shake of the wiseacres' heads and their superior smiles, and the suggestion of the more scientifically inclined that I am your own "subconscious mind." I shall not be offended by that hypothesis, nor need you.

Of course you are not worried, for if you were I could not write. Your mind has to be placid as a lake on a windless night in order for me to write at all.

Give my love to them.

L E T T E R

23

PASSING TIME

I have been able to do what you so much desired—to find the boy who came out accidentally by drowning.

As you looked at his photograph, I saw it through your eyes, and carried away the memory of the face. I found him wandering about, quite bewildered. When I spoke to him of you and said that you had asked me to help him, he seemed surprised.

I was able to give him a little aid, though he has a friend here—an old man who is nearer to him than I could ever be. He will gradually adjust himself to the new conditions.

The little help I was able to give was in the nature of information. He needed diversion from a too-pressing thought, and I suggested one or two ways of passing time which are both agreeable and instructive.

You wonder at the expression "passing time"? But time exists out here. Wherever there is

•

sequence, there is time. There may come a "time" when all things will exist simultaneously, past, present, and—shall we say future? But so long as past, present, and future are more or less distinct, so long time is. It is nothing but the principle of sequence. Did you fancy it was anything else?

Interiorly, that is, deep within the self, one may find a silent place where all things *seem* to exist in unison; but as soon as the soul even there attempts to examine things separately, then sequence begins.

The union with the All is another matter. That is, or seems to be, timeless; but as soon as one attempts to unite with or to be conscious of things, time is manifest.

LETTER

24

A SHADOWLESS WORLD

I had been here some time before I noticed one of the most marked peculiarities of this world.

One night as I was passing slowly along, I saw a group of persons approaching me. It was very light where they were, because there were so many of them. Suddenly, as I saw this light, a thought came to my mind, a saying from one of the Hermetic books: "Where the light is strongest, there are the shadows deepest." But on looking at these men and women, I saw that *they cast no shadows.*

I hailed the nearest man—you must remember that this was soon after I came out, and when I was still more ignorant than I am now— and I called his attention to this peculiar phenomenon of a shadowless yet brilliantly lighted world. He smiled at my surprise, and said:

"You have not been here long, have you?"

"No."

•

"Then you are not aware that we light our own place? The substance of which our bodies are composed is radiant. How could our forms cast shadows, when light radiates from them in all directions?"

"And in the sunlight?" I asked.

"Oh," he answered, "you know that in the sunlight we cannot be seen at all! The light of the sun is coarse and crude, and it puts out the light of the spirits."

Does it seem strange to you that at this moment I can feel the warmth of that wood fire by which you sit? There is a magic in burning wood. The combustion of coal has quite a different effect upon the psychic atmosphere. If one who had always been blind to visions and insensible to the finer feelings and premonitions of the invisible world would try meditating before a blazing wood fire for an hour or two every day or night, his eyes and other subtler senses might be opened to things of which he had theretofore never even dreamed.

Those Orientals who worship their God with fire are wise and full of visions. The light of burning wax has also a magical effect, though different from that of a wood fire. Sit sometimes in the evening with no light but that of a solitary candle, and see what visions will come from the "Void."

I have not told you anything for a long time about the boy Lionel. He is now much interested in the idea of choosing a family of engineers in which to be born again. The thought is one to which he is always returning.

"Why are you in such a hurry to leave me?" I asked him, the first time he mentioned the subject.

"But I do not feel as if I should be leaving you altogether," he replied. "I could come out to you in dreams."

"Not at first," I told him. "You would be prisoned and blind and deaf for a long time, and you might not be able to come out to me here until after I had also gone back again to the earth."

"Then why not come along with me?" he asked. "Say, Father, why shouldn't we be born as twins?"

The idea was so absurd that I laughed heartily; but Lionel could not see where the joke came in.

"There are such things as twins," he said, seriously. "I knew a pair of twin brothers when I lived in Boston."

But, when I return to earth, it is no part of my plan to be anybody's twin; so I tell Lionel that if he wants to enjoy my society for a time, he will have to stay quietly where he is.

"But why can't we go back together?" he still asks, "and be cousins or neighbors, at least?"

"Perhaps we can," I tell him, "if you do not spoil everything by an unseemly haste."

It is strange about this boy. Out in this world there is boundless opportunity to work in subtle matter, opportunity to invent and experiment; yet he wants to get his hands on iron and steel. Strange!

Some night I will try to bring the boy to pay you a visit, so that you can see him—I mean just before you fall asleep. Those are the true visions. The ones which come in sleep are apt to be confused by the jarring of the matter through which you pass in waking. Do not forget the boy. I have already told him how I come and write with your hand, and he is much interested.

"Why couldn't I operate a telegraph in that way?" he asked me; but I advised him not to try it. He might interrupt some terrestrial message which had been sent and paid for.

Occasionally I take him with me up to the pattern world. He has a little model of his own there with which he amuses himself while I am examining other things. It is the model of a wheel, and he sets it going by the electricity of his fingers. No, it is not made of steel—not as you know steel. Why, what you call steel is too heavy! It would fall through this world so fast that it would not even leave a rent behind it.

You must understand that the two worlds are composed of matter not only moving at a different rate of vibration, but charged with a different magnetism. It is said that two solid objects cannot occupy the same space at the same time; but that law does not apply to two objects—one of them belonging to your world and the other to ours. As water can be hot and wet at the same time, so a square foot of space can contain a square foot of earthly matter and a square foot of etheric matter.

No, do not quibble about terms. You have no terms for the kind of matter that we use here, because you do not know anything about it. Lionel and his electric wheel would both be invisible to you if they were set down on the hearth-rug before you at this moment. Even the magic of that wood fire would not make them visible—at least, not in the daylight.

Some evening—but we will speak of that at another time. I must go now.

LETTER
25

CIRCLES IN THE SAND

I am just beginning to enjoy the romance of life out here. I must always have had the romantic temperament; but only since changing my place have I had time and opportunity to give rein to it. On earth there was always too much to be done, too many duties, too many demands on me. Here I am free.

You have no idea of the meaning of freedom unless you can remember when you were out here last, and I doubt if you can remember that yet.

When I say "romance," I mean the charm of existence, the magic touch which turns the gray face of life to rose color. You know what I mean.

It is wonderful to have leisure to dream and to realize one's dream, for here the realization goes with the dream. Everything is so real, imagination is so potent, and the power to link things is so great—so almost unlimited!

The dreamers here are really not idle, for our

dreaming is a kind of building; and even if it were not, we have a right to do about as we please. We have earned our vacation. The labor will come again. We shall reclothe ourselves in gross matter and take on its burdens.

Why, it takes more energy on earth to put one heavy foot before another heavy foot, and to propel the hundred or two-hundred pound body a mile, than it takes here to go around the world! That will give you an idea of the quantity of surplus energy that we have for enjoying ourselves and for dream-building.

Perhaps on earth you work too much—more than is really necessary. The mass of needless things that you accumulate round you, the artificial wants that you create, the breakneck pace of your lives to provide all these things, seem to us absurd and rather pitiful. Your political economy is mere child's play, your governments are cumbrous machines for doing the unnecessary, most of your work is useless, and your lives would be nearly futile if you did not suffer so much that your souls learn, though unwillingly, that most of their strivings are vain.

How I used to sweat and groan in the early days to make my little circle in the sand! And now I see that if I had taken more time to think, I might have recovered something of my past knowledge, gained in other lives; and though I

still had felt obliged to draw my circle in the
sand, I might have done it with less difficulty and
in half the time.

Here, if I choose, I can spend hours in watching the changing colors of a cloud. Or, better still,
I can lie on my back and remember. It is wonderful to remember, to let the mind go back year
after year, life after life, century after century,
back and back till one finds oneself—a turtle! But
one can also look ahead, forward and forward,
life after life, century after century, eon after eon,
till one finds oneself an archangel. The looking
back is memory; the looking forward is creation.
Of course we create our own future. Who else
could do it? We are influenced and moved and
shifted and helped or retarded by others; but it is
we ourselves who forge the chains every time.
We tie knots that we shall have to untie, often
with labor and perplexity.

In going back over my past lives, I realize
the why and the wherefore of my last one. It
was, in a way, the least satisfactory of many
lives—save one; but now I see its purpose, and
that I laid the plans for it when I was last out
here. I even arranged to go back to earth at a
definite time, in order to be with certain friends
who met me there.

But I have turned the corner now, and have
begun the upward march again. Already I am

laying the lines for my next coming, though there is no hurry. Bless you! I am not going back until I have had my fill of the freedom and enjoyment of this existence here.

Also I have much studying to do. I want to review what I learned in those hitherto forgotten but now remembered lives.

Do you recall how, when you went to school, you had occasionally to review the lessons of the preceding weeks or months? That custom is based on a sound principle. I am now having my review lessons. By and by, before I return to the world, I shall review these reviews, fixing by will the memories which I specially wish to carry over with me. It would be practically impossible to carry over intact the great panorama of experience which now unrolls itself before the eyes of my memory; but there are several fundamental things, philosophical principles and illustrations, which I must not forget. Also I want to take with me the knowledge of certain formulae and the habit of certain practices which you would probably call occult; by means of which, when I am mature again in my new body, I can call into memory this very pageant of experience which now rolls before me whenever I will it.

No, I am not going to tell you about your own past. You must, and can, recover it for yourself. So can anyone who knows the difference between memory and imagination. Yes, the difference is subtle, but as real as the difference between yesterday and tomorrow.

I do not want you to be in any hurry about coming out here to stay. Remain where you are just as long as possible. Much that we do on this side you can do almost as well while still in the body. Of course you have to use more energy, but that is what energy is for—to use. Even when we store it, we store it for future use. Do not forget that.

One reason why I rest much now and dream and amuse myself is because I want to store as much energy as possible, to come back with power.

It is well that you have taken my advice to idle a little and to get acquainted with your own soul. There are surprises in store for the person who will deliberately set out on the quest of his soul. The soul is not a will-o'-the-wisp; it is a beacon light to steer by and avoid the rocks of materialism and forgetfulness.

I have had much joy in going back over my Greek incarnations. What concentration they had—those Greeks! They knew much. The waters of Lethe, for instance—what a conception!—brought from this side by masterly memory.

If man would even try to remember, if he would only take time to consider all that he has been, there would be more hope of what he may become! Why, do you know that man may become a god—or that which, compared with ordinary humanity, has all the magnitude and grandeur of a god? "Ye are gods," was not said in a merely figurative sense.

I have met the Master of Galilee, and have held communion with Him. There was a man—and a god! The world has need of Him now.

L E T T E R
26

The Magic Ring

It would be hard for you to understand, merely by my telling you, the difference between your life and ours. Begin with the difference in substance, not only the substance of our bodies, but the substance of natural objects which surround us.

Do you start at the term "natural objects" as applied to the things of this world? You did not fancy, did you, that we had escaped Nature? No one escapes Nature—not even God. Nature *is*.

Imagine that you had spent sixty or seventy years in a heavy earthly body, a body which insisted on growing fat, and would get stiff-jointed and rheumatic, even going on strike occasionally to the extent of laying you up in bed for repairs of a more or less clumsy sort. Then fancy yourself suddenly exchanging this heavy body for a light and elastic form. Can you imagine it? I confess that it would have been difficult for me, even a year or two ago.

Clothed in this form, which is sufficiently radiant to light its own place when its light is not put out by the cruder light of the sun, fancy yourself moving from place to place, from person to person, from idea to idea. As time goes on even the habit of demanding nourishment gradually wears off. We are no longer bothered by hunger and thirst; though I, for instance, still stay myself occasionally with a little nourishment, an infinitesimal amount compared with the beefsteak dinners which I used to eat.

And we are no longer harassed by the thousand-and-one petty duties of the earth. Out here we have more confidence in moods. Engagements are seldom made—that is, binding engagements. As a rule, though there are exceptions, desire is mutual. I want to see and commune with a friend at the same time when he feels a desire for my society, and we naturally drift together. The companionships here are very beautiful, but the solitudes are also full of charm.

Since the first two or three months I have not been lonesome. At first I felt like a fish out of water, of course. Nearly everyone does; though there are exceptions in the case of very spiritual people who have no earthly ties or ambitions. I had so fought the idea of "dying," that my new state seemed at first to be the proof of my failure, and I used to wander about under the impression that I was going to waste much valuable time which could have been used to better advantage in the storm and stress of earthly living.

Of course the Teacher came to me; but he was too wise to carry me on his back even from the first. He reminded me of a few principles, which he left me to apply; and gradually, as I got hold of the applications, I got hold of myself. Then also gradually the beauty and wonder of the new condition began to dawn on me, and I saw that instead of wasting time I was really gaining tremendous experience which could be utilized later.

I have talked with many people here, people of all stages of intellectual and moral growth, and I am sorry to say that the person who has a clear idea of the significance of life and its possibilities for development is about as rare here as on the earth. As I have said before, a man does not suddenly become all-wise by changing the texture of his body.

The vain man of earth is likely to be vain here, though in his next life the very law of reaction—if he has overdone vanity—may send him back as a modest or even bashful person, for a while at least, until the reaction has spent itself. In coming out a man brings his character and characteristics with him.

I have often been sorry for men who in life had been slaves of the business routine. Many of them cannot get away from it for a long time; and instead of enjoying themselves here, they go back and forth to and from the scenes of their old labors, working over and over some problem in tactics or finance until they are almost as weary as when they "died."

As you know, there are teachers here. Few of them are of the stature of my own Teacher; but there are many who make it their pleasure to help the souls of the newly arrived. They never leave a newcomer entirely to his own resources. Help is always offered, though it is not always accepted. In that case it will be offered again and again, for those who give themselves to others do so without hope of reward or even acknowledgment.

If I had set out to write a scientific treatise of the life on this side, I should have begun in quite a different way from this. In the first place, I should have postponed the labor about ten years, until all my facts were pigeonholed and docketed; then I should have begun at the beginning and dictated a book so dull that you would have fallen asleep over it, and I should have had to nudge you from time to time to pick up the pencil fallen from your somnolent hand.

•

Instead, I began to write soon after coming out, and these letters are really the letters of a traveler in a strange country. They record his impressions, often his mistakes, sometimes perhaps his provincial prejudices; but at least they are not a rehash of what somebody else has said.

I like your keeping my photograph on your mantel as you do; it helps me to come. There is a great power in a photograph.

I have been drawing pictures for you lately on the canvas of dreams, to show you the futility and vanity of certain things. Did you not know that we could do that? The power of the so-called dead to influence the living is immense, provided that the tie of sympathy has been made. I have taught you how to protect yourself against influences which you do not want, so do not be afraid. I will always stand guard to the extent of warning you if there is any threat of intrusion from this side. Already I have drawn a magic ring around you which only the most advanced and powerful spirits could pass, even if they desired—that is, the Teachers and I drew it together. You are doing our work just now, and have a right to our protection. That the laborer is worthy of his hire is an axiom of both worlds.

106

Only you yourself could now let down the bars for the inrush of irresponsible spiritual intelligences, and if you should inadvertently let down the bars, we should rush to put them up again. We have some authority out here. Yes, even so soon I can say that. Are you surprised?

L E T T E R

27

EXCEPT YE BE AS LITTLE CHILDREN

I once heard a man refer to this world as the play world, "for," said he, "we are all children here, and we create the environment that we desire." As a child at play can turn a chair into a tower or a prancing steed, so we in this world can make real for the moment whatever we imagine.

Has it never filled you with amazement, that absolute vividness of the imagination of children? A child says unblushingly and with conviction, "That rug is a garden, that plank in the floor is a river, that chair is a castle, and I am a king."

Why does he say these things? How *can* he say these things? Because—and here is the point—he still subconsciously remembers the life out here which he so lately left. He has carried over with him into the life of earth something of his lost freedom and power of imagination.

That does not mean that all things in this world are imaginary—far from it. Objects here, objects existing in tenuous matter, are as real and comparatively substantial as with you; but there is the possibility of creation here, creation in a form of matter even more subtle still—thought-substance.

If you create something on earth in solid matter, you create it first in thought-substance; but there is this difference between your creation and ours: until you have molded solid matter around your thought-pattern, you do not believe that the thought-pattern really exists save in your own fancy.

We out here can see the thought-creations of others if we and they will it so.

We can also—and I tell you this for your comfort—we can also see your thought-creations, and by adding the strength of our will to yours, we can help you to realize them in substantial form.

Sometimes we build here bit by bit, in the four-dimensional world, especially when we wish to leave a thing for others to see and enjoy, when we wish a thing to survive for a long time. But a thought-form is visible to all highly developed spirits.

Of course you understand that not all spirits are highly developed. In fact, very few are far progressed; but the dullest man out here has something which most of you have lost—the faith in his own thought-creations.

Now, the power which makes creation possible is not lost to a soul when it takes on solid matter again. But the power is gradually overcome and the imagination is discouraged by the incredulity of mature men and women, who say constantly to the child: "That is only play; that is not really so; that is only imagination."

If you print these letters, I wish you would insert here fragments from the wonderful poem of Wordsworth, "Intimations of Immortality from Recollections of Early Childhood."

> Our birth is but a sleep and a forgetting;
> The Soul that rises with us, our life's Star,
>   Hath had elsewhere its setting,
>   And cometh from afar:
>   Not in entire forgetfulness,
>   And not in utter nakedness,
> But trailing clouds of glory do we come
>   From God, who is our home:
> Heaven lies about us in our infancy!
> Shades of the prison-house begin to close
>   Upon the growing Boy,
> But he beholds the light, and whence it flows,
>   He sees it in his joy;
> The Youth, who daily farther from the east
>   Must travel, still is Nature's Priest,
>   And by the vision splendid
>   Is on his way attended;
> At length the Man perceives it die away,
> And fade into the light of common day.

There is almost no limit to the possibilities of the imagination; but to get the full power of it, one must trust one's imagination. If you say to yourself constantly, as the mother says to the child, "But this is only play; this is not real," you never can make real the things you have created in thought.

The imagination itself is like a child and must be encouraged and believed in, or it cannot develop and do its perfect work.

It is really fortunate for some of you that I am out here. I can do more for you here than there, because I have even greater faith in my imagination than I had before.

The man who called this the play world has been trying all sorts of experiments with the power in himself. I have not his permission to tell the stories he tells me, but they would surprise you. For one thing, he helped his wife, after his so-called death, to carry out a joint plan of theirs which had seemed impossible to them before because of their lack of real faith. It was for the erection of a certain kind of house.

But do not fancy that most people here are trying to build houses on earth. Far from it. Most of my fellow citizens are willing to work where they are, and to let the earth alone. Of course there are "dreamers" like me, who are not satisfied with one world, and who like to have their

111

fingers in both; but they are rather rare, as poets are rare on earth. To most men the world they happen to be in is sufficient for the time being.

There is a certain fancy of mine, however, which it will amuse me to help realize on earth. You may not know that I am doing it, but I shall know. I would not, "for the world," as you say, disturb anybody by even the thought that I am fussing around in affairs which now are theirs. But if, unseen and unfelt, I can help with the power of my self-confident imagination, there will be no harm done, and I shall have demonstrated something.

L E T T E R
28

An Unexpected Warning

I should be very sorry if the reading of these letters of mine should cause foolish and unthinking people to go spirit-hunting, inviting into their human sphere the irresponsible and often deceitful elemental spirits. Tell them not to do it.

My coming in this way through your hand is quite another matter. I could not do it if I had not been instructed in the scientific method of procedure, and I also could not do it if you should constantly interrupt me by side-thoughts of your own, and by questions relevant or irrelevant. It is because you are perfectly passive and not even curious, letting me use your hand as on earth I would have used the hand of my stenographer, that I am able to write long and connected sentences.

Most spirit communications, even when genuine, have little value, for the reason that they are nearly always colored by the mind of the person through whom they pass.

You are right in reading nothing on the subject while these messages are coming, and in thinking nothing about this plane of life where I am. Thus you avoid preconceived ideas, which would interrupt the flow of *my* ideas.

You know, perhaps, that while on earth I investigated spiritualism, as I investigated many things of an occult nature, looking always for the truth that was behind them; but I was convinced then, and I am now more than ever convinced, that, except for the scientific demonstration that *such things can be*—which, of course, has value as a demonstration only—most spirit-hunting is not only a waste of time, but an absolute detriment to those who engage in it.

This may sound strange coming from a so-called "spirit," one who is actually at this time in communication with the world. If that is so, I cannot help it. If I seem inconsistent, then I seem so; that is all. But I wish to go on record as discouraging irresponsible mediumship.

If a person sitting for mediumship could be sure that at the other end of the psychic line there was an entity who had something sincere and important to say, and who really could use him or her to say it through, it would be another matter; but this world out here is full of vagrants, even as the earth. As this world is peopled largely from your world, it is inevitable that we have the same kind of beings that you have. They have not changed much in passing through the doors of death.

Would you advise any delicate and sensitive woman to sit down in the center of Hyde Park, and invite the passing crowds to come and speak through her, or touch her, or mingle their magnetism with hers? You shudder. You would shudder more had you seen some of the things which I have seen.

Then, too, there is another class of beings here, the kind which we used to hear the Theosophists call elementals. Now, there has been a lot of nonsense written about elementals; but take this for a fact: there are units of energy, units of consciousness, which correspond pretty closely to what the Theosophists understand by elementals. These entities are not, as a rule, very highly developed; but as the stage of earth life is the stage to which they aspire, and as it is the next inevitable stage in their evolution, they are drawn to it powerfully.

So do not be too sure that the entity which raps on your table or your cupboard is the spirit of your deceased grandfather. It may be merely a blind and very *desirous* entity, an eager consciousness, trying to use you to hasten its own evolution, trying to get into you or through you, so as to enjoy the earth and the coarser vibrations of the earth.

115

●

It may not be able to harm you; but, on the other hand, it may do you a great deal of harm. You had better discourage such attempts to break through the veil which separates you from them; for the veil is thinner than you think, and though you cannot see through it, you can feel through it.

Having said this, my duty in the matter is discharged; and the next time I come I can tell you a story, maybe, instead of giving you a lecture.

I really feel like an astral Scheherazade; but I fear you would tire of me before a thousand-and-one nights were past. A thousand-and-one nights! Before that time I shall have gone on. No, I do not mean "died" again into another world beyond; but when I get through telling you what I desire you to know about my life here, I want to investigate other stars, if it shall be permitted.

I am like a young man who has lately inherited a fortune and has at last unlimited means and opportunity for travel. Though he might stay around home a few months, getting matters in shape and becoming adjusted to his new freedom of movement, yet the time would come when he would want to try his wings. I hope that is not a mixed metaphor; if so, you can edit me. I shall not feel hurt.

LETTER
29

The Sylph and the Magician

If your eyes could pierce the veil of matter, and you could see what goes on in the tenuous world around and above that city of Paris, you would gasp with wonder. I have spent much time in Paris lately. Shall I tell you some of the strange things I have seen?

In a street on the left bank of the river, called the *rue de Vaugirard*, there lives a man of middle age and sedentary habits who is a sort of magician. He is constantly attended and served by one of the elemental spirits known as sylphs. This sylph he calls Meriline. I do not know from what language he got the name, for he seems to speak several, and to know Hebrew. I have seen this Meriline coming and going to and from his apartment. No, it would not be right for me to tell you where it is. The man could be identified, though the sylph would elude the census-taker.

Meriline does not make his bed or cook his broth, for which humble service he has a charwoman; but the sylph runs errands and discovers things for him. He is a collector of old books and manuscripts, and many of his treasures have been located by Meriline in the stalls which lie along the banks of the Seine, and also in more pretentious bookshops.

This man is not a devil-worshiper. He is only a harmless enthusiast, fond of occult things, and striving to pierce the veil which shuts the elemental world from his eyes. A little less brandy and wine, and he *might* be able to see clearly, for he is a true student. But he is fond of the flesh, and it preys upon the spirit.

One day I encountered Meriline going upon one of his errands, and I introduced myself by signaling with my hands and calling my name. This attracted the attention of the sprite, who came and stood beside me.

"Where are you going?" I asked; and she nodded towards the other side of the river.

The thought came to me that perhaps I ought not to question this servant of the good magician as to her master's business, so I hesitated. She also hesitated; then she said:

"But he is interested in the spirits of men."

This made the matter simpler, and I asked:

"You do his errands?"

"Yes, always."

"Why do you do his errands?"

"Because I love to serve him."

"And why do you love to serve him?"

"Because I belong to him."

"I thought every soul belonged to itself."

"But I am not a soul!"

"Then what are you?"

"A sylph."

"Do you ever expect to be a soul?"

"Oh, yes! He has promised that I shall be, if I serve him faithfully."

"But how can he make you to be a soul?"

"I don't know; but he will."

"How do you know that he will?"

"Because I trust him."

"What makes you trust him?"

"Because he trusts me."

"And you always tell him the truth?"

"Always."

"Who taught you what truth is?"

"He did."

"How?"

This seemed to puzzle the being before me, and I feared she would go away; so I detained her by saying, quickly:

"I do not want to worry you with questions which you cannot answer. Tell me how you first came into his service."

"Ought I?"

"So you have a conscience?"

•

"Yes, he taught me to have."

"But you say that he is interested in the spirits of men."

"Yes, and I also know good spirits from bad ones."

"Did he teach you that?"

"No."

"How did you learn?"

"I always knew."

"Then you have lived a long time?"

"Oh, yes!"

"And when do you expect to have, or to become, a soul?"

"When he comes out here, into this world where we are."

This staggered me by its daring. Had the good magician been deceiving his sylph, or did he really believe what he promised?"

"What did he say about it?" I asked.

"That if I would serve him now, he would serve me later."

"And how is he going to do it?"

"I don't know."

"Suppose you ask him?"

"I never ask questions. I answer them."

"For instance, what sort of questions?"

"I tell him where such and such a person is, and what he or she is doing."

"Can you tell him what these people are thinking?"

"Not often—or not always. Sometimes I can."

"How can you tell?"

"By the feel of them. If I am warm in their presence, I know they are friendly to him; if I am cold, I know they are his enemies. If I feel nothing at all, then I know that they are not thinking of him, or are indifferent."

"And your errand this evening?"

"To see a lady."

"And you are not jealous?"

"What is 'jealous'?"

"You are not displeased that he should interest himself in ladies?"

"Why should I be?"

This was a question I could not answer, not knowing the nature of sylphs. She surprised me a little, for I had supposed that all female beings were jealous. But, fearing again that she might leave me, I hurried to question her further.

"How did you make his acquaintance?" I asked.

"He called me."

"How?"

"By the incantation."

"What incantation?"

"The call to the sylphs."

"Oh," I said, "he called the sylphs and you came!"

•

"Yes, of course. I liked him for his kindness, and I made him see me."

"How did you manage it?"

"I dazzled his eyes until he closed them, and then he could see me."

"Can he always see you now?"

"No, but he knows I am there."

"He can see you sometimes still?"

"Yes, often."

"And when he saw you first?"

"He was delighted, and called me loving names, and made me promises."

"The promise of a soul—that first time?"

"Yes."

122

"Then you had wanted to have a soul?"

"Oh, yes!"

"But why?"

"Many of us want to be men. We love men—that is, most of us do."

"Why do you love men?"

"It is our nature."

"But not the nature of all of you?"

"There are malignant spirits of the air."

"And what will you do when you have a soul?"

"I will take a body, and live on earth."

"And leave your friend whom you now serve?"

"Oh, no! It is to be with him that I specially want a body."

•

"Then will he come back to the earth with you?"

"He says so."

This again staggered me. I was becoming interested in this magician; he had a daring imagination.

Could a spirit of the air develop into a human soul? I asked myself. Was the man self-deceived? Or, again, was he deceiving his lovely messenger?

I thought a little too long this time, for when I turned again to speak to my strange companion, she had left me. I tried to follow, but could not find her; and if she returned soon, it must have been by some other road. Though I looked in all directions, she was invisible to me.

Now, the question will arise in your mind: In what language did I talk with this aerial servant of a French magician? I seemed to speak in my own tongue, and she seemed to respond in the same. How is that? I cannot say, unless we really used the subtle language of thought itself.

You may often, on meeting with a person whose language you do not speak, feel an interchange of ideas, by the look of the eyes, by the expression of the face, by gestures. Now imagine that intensified a hundredfold. Might it not extend to the simple questions and answers which I exchanged with the sylph? I do not say that it would, but I think it might; for, as I said before, I seemed to speak and she seemed to reply in my own language.

What strange experiences one has out here! I rather dread to go back into the world, where it will be so dull for me for a long time. Can I exchange this freedom and vivid life for a long period of somnolence, afterwards to suck a bottle and learn the multiplication table and Greek and Latin verbs? I suppose I must—but not yet.

Good night.

124

•

L E T T E R
30

A Problem in
Celestial Mathematics

By the vividness with which you feel my presence at times, you can judge of the intensity of the life that I am living. I am no pallid spook, dripping with grave-dew. I am real, and quite as wholesome—or so it seems to me—as when I walked the earth in a more or less unhealthy body.

It would have been amazing had you been afraid of me. But there are those who would be, if they should sense my presence as you sense it.

One night I knocked at the door of a friend's chamber, half expecting a welcome. He jumped out of bed in alarm, then jumped back again, and pulled the blanket over his head. He was really afraid that it might be I! So, as I did not wish to be responsible for a case of heart failure, or for a shock of hair which, like that in the old song, "turned white in a single night," I went quietly away. Doubtless he persuaded himself next day that there were mice in the wainscotting.

•

Had you been afraid of me, though, I should have been ashamed of you; for you know better. Most persons do not.

It is a real pleasure for me to come back and talk with you sometimes. "There are no friends like the old friends," and the society of sylphs and spirits would never quite satisfy me if all those whom I had known and loved should turn their backs on me.

Speaking of sylphs, I met the Teacher last night, and asked him if that French magician I told you about could really make good his promise to his aerial companion, and help her to acquire the kind of soul essential to incarnation on earth as a woman. His answer was, "No."

Of course I asked him why, and he answered that the elemental creatures, or units of force inhabiting the elements, as we use that term, could not, during this life cycle, step out of their element into the human.

"Can they ever do so?" I asked.

"I do not know," he replied; "but I believe that all the less evolved units around the earth are working in the direction of man; that the human is a stage of development which they will all reach some day, but not in this life cycle."

I asked the Teacher if he knew the magician in question, and he answered that he had known him for a thousand years, that long ago, in a former life, the Paris magician had placed his feet upon the path which leads to power; but that he had been sidetracked by the desire for selfish pleasures, and that he might wander a long time before he found his way back to real and philosophical truth.

"Is he to be blamed or pitied?" I asked.

"Pity cuts no figure in the problem," the Teacher replied. "A man seeks what he desires."

After the Teacher went away, I began asking myself questions. What was *I* seeking, and what did I desire? The answer came quickly: "Knowledge." A year ago I might have answered "Power," but knowledge is the forerunner of power. If I get true knowledge, I shall have power enough.

It is because I want to give to you, and possibly to others, a few scraps of knowledge which might be inaccessible to you by any other means, that I am coming back, and coming back, time after time, to talk with you.

The greatest bit of knowledge that I have to offer you is this: that by the exercise of will a man can retain his objective consciousness after death. Many persons out here sink into a sort of subjective bliss which makes them indifferent as to what is going on upon the earth or in the heavens. I could do so myself, easily.

•

As I believe I have said before, while man on earth has both subjective and objective consciousness, but functions mostly in the objective, out here he has still subjective and objective consciousness, but the tendency is towards the subjective.

At almost any time, on composing yourself and looking in, you can fall into a state of subjective bliss which is similar to that enjoyed by souls on this side of the dividing line called death. In fact, it is by such subconscious experience that man has learned nearly all he knows regarding the etheric world. When the storms and passions of the body are stilled, man can catch a glimpse of his own interior life, and that interior life is the life of this fourth-dimensional plane. Please do not accuse me of contradicting myself or of being obscure; I have said that the objective consciousness is as possible with us as the subjective is with you, but that the tendency is merely the other way.

You may remember a pair of lovers about whom I wrote you a few weeks ago. He had been out here some time, and had waited for her, and helped her over the uncertain marshlands which lie between the two states of existence.

I saw these lovers again the other day, but they were not at all excited by my appearance. On the contrary, I fancy that I put them out

128

•

somewhat by awakening them, by calling them back from the state of subjective bliss into which they have sunk since being together at last.

While he waited for her all those years, he kept himself awake by expectation; while still on earth she was always thinking of him out here, and so the polarity was sustained. Now they have each other; they are in "the little home" which he built for her with so much pleasure out of the tenuous materials of this tenuous world; they see each other's faces whether they look out or in; they are content; they have nothing more to attain (or so they tell each other), and they consequently sink back into the arms of subjective bliss.

129

Now this state of bliss, of rumination, they have a right to enjoy. No one can take it from them. They have earned it by activity in the world and elsewhere; it is theirs by rhythmic justice. They will enjoy it, I fancy, for a long time, living over the past experiences which they have had together and apart. Then some day one or the other of them will become surfeited with too much sweetness; the muscles of his (or her) soul will stretch for want of exercise; he (or she) will give a spiritual yawn, and by the law of reaction, pass out—not to return.

Where will he (or she) go, you ask? Why, back to the earth, of course!

•

Let us imagine him (or her) awakening from that subjective state of bliss which is known to them as attainment, and going for a short promenade in blessed and wholesome solitude. Then, with a sort of morning alertness in the heart and the eye, he (or she) draws near to a pair of earthly lovers. Suddenly the call of matter, the eager, terrible call of blood and warmth, of activity raised to the nth power, catches the half-awakened soul on the ethereal side of matter and ——

He has again entered the world of material formation. He is sunk and hidden in the flesh of earth. He awaits birth. He will come out with great force, by reason of his former rest. He might even become a "captain of industry," if he is a strong unit. But I began by saying "he or she." Let me change the figure. The man would be almost certain to awake first, by reason of his positive polarity.

Now, in drawing this imaginary picture of my lovers, I am not making a dogma of the way in which all souls return to earth. I am merely guessing how these two will return (for she would probably follow him speedily when she awoke and found herself alone). And the reason why I fancy they will return in that way is because they are indulging themselves in too much subjective bliss.

When will they go back? I cannot say. Perhaps next year, perhaps in a hundred years. Not knowing the numerical value of their unit of force, I cannot guess how much subjective bliss they can endure without a violent reaction.

I am sure that you are wondering if some day I shall myself sink into that state of bliss which I have described. Perhaps. I should enjoy it—but not for long, and not yet. However, I have no sweetheart out here to enjoy it with me.

L E T T E R
31

A CHANGE OF FOCUS

With the guidance of the Teacher, during the last few weeks I have been going to and fro in the earth and walking up and down in it. You smile at the veiled reference. But have not certain friends of yours actually feared me, as if I were the devil of the Book of Job?

Now, to be serious, I have been visiting those lands and cities where in former lives I lived and worked among men. One of the many advantages of travel is that it helps a man to remember his former existences. There is certainly a magic in places.

I have been in Egypt, in India, in Persia, in Spain, in Italy; I have been in Germany, Switzerland, Austria, Greece, Turkey, and many other lands. The Dardanelles were not closed to me recently, when by reason of the war you could not have passed through. There are advantages to almost every condition, even my present one; for the law of compensation holds good.

•

In certain lives of the past I was a wide traveler.

Now you may wonder how it is that I pass easily from this world to yours, seeing into both. But you must remember that your world and mine occupy about the same space; that the plane of the earth's surface is one of the lower and more material planes of our world, using the word "plane" as you would use the word "layer."

As I have said before, there are also places accessible to us which lie at some distance above the earth's surface. "Mansions in the skies" are more than figurative.

I have only slightly to change my focus at any time, to find myself in your world. That I cannot be seen there with the naked eye is no proof that I am not there. Without that change of focus, which is done through an action of will and by knowing the method, I might even be occupying the same space as something in your world and not know it. Note well this point, for it is only half of something which I have to say. The other half is, that you also may at any time be—so far as space is concerned—in the immediate neighborhood of interesting things in our world, and not know that you are there.

But if you focus to this world, you are more or less conscious of it. So when I, knowing how, focus to your world, I am there in consciousness and can enjoy the varied sights of many cities, the changing aspects of many lands.

When I first came out, I could not see my way about the earth very well, but now I can see better.

No, I am not going to give you a formula to give to other people by which you or they could change focus at will and enter into relation with this world, because such knowledge at the present stage of human progress would do more harm than good. I merely state the fact, and leave the application for those who have the curiosity and the ability to demonstrate it.

My object in writing these letters is primarily to convince a few persons—to strengthen their certainty in the fact of immortality, or the survival of the soul after the bodily change which is called death. Many think they believe who are not certain whether they believe or not. If I can make my presence as a living and vital entity felt in these letters, it will have the effect of strengthening the belief of certain persons in the doctrine of immortality.

This is a materialistic age. A large percentage of men and women have no real interest in the life beyond the grave. But they will all have to come out here sooner or later, and perhaps a few will find the change easier, the journey less formidable, by reason of what I shall have taught them. Is it not worthwhile? Is it not worth a little effort on your part as well as on mine?

Any person approaching the great change who shall seriously study these letters and lay their principles to heart, and who shall will to remember them after passing out, need not fear anything.

We all fail in much that we undertake, but I hope I shall not fail in this. Do not you fail on your side. I could not do this work without you, nor could you do it without me. That is in answer to the supposition that I am your subconscious mind.

I have been in Constantinople and have stood in the very room where I once had a remarkable experience, hundreds of years ago. I have seen the walls, I have touched them, I have read the etheric records of their history, and my own history in connection therewith.

I have walked the rose gardens of Persia and have smelled the flowers—the grandchildren, hundreds of times removed, of those roses whose fragrance was an ecstasy to me when, watching with the bulbul, I paced there in another form and with intentions different to mine now. It was the perfume of the roses which made me remember.

In Greece also I have lived over the old days. Before their degeneration began, what a race they were! I think that concentration was the secret of their power. The ether around that peninsula is written over with their exploits, in daring thought as well as daring action. The old etheric records are so vivid that they shine through the later writings; for you must know that what are called astral records lie layer against layer everywhere. We read one layer instead of another, either by affinity or by will. It is no more strange than that a man may go among the millions of volumes in the British Museum and select the one he wants. The most marvelous things are always simple of explanation if one has the key to unlock their secret.

136

There has been much nonsense written about vibration, but nevertheless truth lies thereabouts. Where there is so much smoke there must be fire.

In India I have met with yogis in meditation. Do you know why their peculiar way of breathing produces psychic results? No, you do not. Now let me tell you: By holding the breath long a certain—shall I say poison?—is produced in the body, which poison, acting on the psychic nature, changes the vibration. That is all. Volumes have been written about yoga, but have any of them said that? The untrained healthy lungs, in ordinary operation, get rid of this poison by processes well known to physiolo-

•

gists—that is, in the natural man, adjusted to and working contentedly on the material plane. But in order for a man still living on the material plane to become adjusted to the psychic world, a change of vibration is necessary. This change of vibration may be produced by a slight overdose of the above-mentioned poison. Is it dangerous? Yes, to the ignorant. To those who are learned in its use it is no more dangerous than most of the drugs in the pharmacopoeia.

Another time I will tell you about other secrets which I have discovered going to and fro in the earth and walking up and down in it.

137

•

LETTER

32

FIVE RESOLUTIONS

I have stood at night on the roof of an Oriental palace and watched the stars. You who can see into the invisible world by changing your focus can easily understand how I, by a reverse process, can see into the world of dense matter. Yes, it is the same thing, only turned the other way.

I stood on the roof of an Oriental palace and watched the stars. No mortal was near me. Looking down upon the sleeping city, I have seen the cloud of souls which kept watch above it, have seen the messengers coming and going. Once or twice a wan, half-frightened face appeared among the cloud of spirits, and I knew that down below in the city someone had died.

But I had seen so many spirits since coming out here that I was more interested in watching the stars. I used to love them, and I love them still. Some day, if it is permitted, I hope to know more about them. But I shall not leave the neighborhood of the earth until these letters are finished. From the distance of the planet Jupiter I might not be able to write at all. It is true that one can come and go, almost with the quickness of thought; but something tells me that it is better to postpone for a time my more extensive traveling. Perhaps when I get out there I shall not want to come back for a long time.

It means much to me, this correspondence with earth. During my illness I used to wonder if I could come back sometimes, but I never imagined anything like this. I would not have supposed it possible to find any well-balanced and responsible person with daring enough to join me in the experiment.

I could not have written through the hand of a person of untrained mind unless he or she had been fully hypnotized. I could not have written through the hand of the average intellectual person, because such persons cannot make themselves sufficiently passive.

Be at peace. You are not a spirit medium, using the word as it is commonly used, signifying a passive instrument, an aeolian harp, set in an aperture between the two worlds and played upon by any wind that blows.

Except as illustrating the fact that it can be done, there is no great object in my telling you

139

of the things I have seen in your world since coming to this other one. The next time you look out into this plane of life and see the wonderful landscapes and the people, remember that it is in a similar way that I look back into your plane of existence. It is interesting to live in two worlds, going back and forth at will. But when I go into yours, it is only as a visitor, and I shall never attempt to take a hand in its government. There is such a rigorous custom-house on the frontier between the two worlds that the traveler back and forth cannot afford to carry anything with him—not even prejudice.

If you should come out here with a determination to see only certain things, you might give a wrong value to what you would see. Many have come out here at death with that mental attitude, and so have learned little or nothing. It is the traveler with the open mind who makes discoveries.

I brought over with me only a few resolutions:

To preserve my identity;

To hold my memory of earth life, and to carry back the memory of this life when I should return to the world;

To see the great Teachers;

To recover the memories of my past incarnations;

To lay the necessary foundations for a great earth life when I should go back next time.

•

That sounds simple, does it not? Already I have done much besides; but if I had not borne these points in mind, I might have accomplished little.

The only really sad thing about death is that the average man learns so little from it. Only my realization of the fact that the chain of earth lives is relatively endless could keep me from regret that most persons make so little progress in each life. But I comfort myself with the assurance that there is no hurry; that the pearls in the chain of existence, though small, are all in their inevitable places, and that the chain is a circle, the symbol of eternity.

And it seems to me, with my still finite view, that most men on this side waste their lives even as they do on your side. That shows how far I am yet from the ideal knowledge.

Viewed from the stars, whence I hope some day to view them, all these flat stretches in the landscape of life may be softened by distance, and the whole picture may take on a perspective of beauty which I had not dreamed of while I myself was but a speck upon the canvas.

L E T T E R

33

THE PASSING OF LIONEL

I have lost my boy Lionel. He has gone— I started to say the way of all flesh; but I must revise the figure and say the way of all spirits, sooner or later, and that way is back to earth.

One day not long ago I found him absorbed in thought in our favorite resting place, the little hut beside a stream at the foot of a wooded hill, which I told you about in one of my former letters.

I waited for a time until the boy opened his eyes and looked at me.

"Father," he said, "my favorite teacher is going to be married tomorrow."

"How do you know?" I asked.

"Why, I have been listening!" he answered. "Every little while I go back and pay her a visit, though she does not know I am there. I have been aware that there was something in the wind."

"Why?"

"Because she has been so shining; there is a light around her which was not there before."

"What caused the light, Lionel?"

"Well, I suppose she is what they call *in love.*"

"You are a phenomenally wise child," I said.

He looked at me with his large, honest eyes.

"I am not really a child at all," he answered. "I am as old as the hills, as you, or as anybody. Have you not told me that we are all immortal, without end or beginning?"

"Yes, but go on, tell me about your teacher."

"She is in love with the big brother of one of my playfellows. I used to know him when I was a little boy. He let me use his magnet, and taught me kite-flying, and showed me how machinery went. He is an engineer."

"Oh!" I said. "In this case, of course you are glad that your favorite teacher is going to marry him."

Lionel's eyes were larger than ever as he said:

"I shall be sorry to leave you, Father; but it is a chance I cannot afford to miss."

"What!"

"It is my opportunity to go back. I've been watching for it a long time."

"But are you ready?"

"What is it to be ready? I *want* to go."

"And leave me?"

•

"I shall find you again. And—Oh, Father!—when you come back, I shall be older than you." This idea seemed to delight him.

I was still human enough to be sorry that the boy was going of his own free will; but as will *is* free, I would not make any effort to detain him. Though young in that form, which had not yet had time to grow up in the tenuous world since he came out as a child, yet he was old in thought.

"Yes," I said, "perhaps you can help me along when I also shall be a child again."

"You see," he went on, "with a father like Victor, I shall learn all I want to know about machinery—that is, all that he can teach me; but when I am grown, I shall find out for myself many things which he does not know. You remember the little machine I have been working with, up in the pattern world?"

"Yes."

"When I am back on the earth, I shall make it a reality. Why, it actually runs now with the electricity from my fingers!"

"But will it, when you have fixed it in material form, in steel, or whatever it is to be made of?"

"Yes, of course it will. It is my invention. I shall be a famous man."

"But supposing that somebody else finds it first?"

"I don't think anybody will."

"Shall I help you to lay a spell around the pattern, so that no one can touch it?"

"Could you do that, Father?"

"I think so."

"Then let us go up there at once," he said, "and do it immediately. I may have to leave this world in a day or two."

I could not help smiling at the boy's desire to hurry. Doubtless he would be present at that wedding, and I should see little or nothing of him afterwards.

We went up to the pattern world, and with his assistance, I drew a circle around the little machine—a spell which, I think, will protect it until he is ready to make his claim.

Oh inspiration! Oh invention! Genius! Little do the men of earth know the meaning of those words. Perhaps the poet's famous poem was sung before his birth; perhaps the engineer's invention lay in the pattern world, protected by his spell, while he grew to manhood and advanced in science and made ready to claim it for his own, his prior and spiritual creation. Perhaps, when two men discover or invent the same thing at about the same time, one has succeeded in appropriating the design which the other left behind him when he came back to earth. Sometimes, perhaps, both have taken from the invisible the creation of a third man, who still awaits rebirth.

Lionel babbled on to me about the life to come, and of what a charming mother Miss —— would be. She had always been good to him.

"Perhaps," I said, "many of us who return almost immediately, as you hope to do, seek out those who have been good to us in a former life."

"There is another point," Lionel said. "Miss —— is a friend of my own mother, the one I left a few years ago. It will be so good to have her hold my hand again."

"Do you think she will recognize you?" I asked.

"Who knows? She believes in rebirth."

"How can you say that? You were so little when you came out!"

"I was seven years old, and already she had told me that we live many lives on earth."

"Bless the souls who first brought that belief to the Western world!" I exclaimed. "And now, my boy, is there anything that I can do for you after you leave me?"

"Yes, of course; you can watch over my new mother, and warn her if any danger threatens her or me."

"Then make me acquainted with her now."

We went out into the material world, the boy and I. Already I have told you how we go.

●

He took me to a little house in one of the suburbs of Boston. We entered a room—it was then about eleven o'clock at night upon that part of the earth—and I saw a fair young woman kneeling beside her bed, praying to God that He would bless the union of the morrow which was to give her to the man she loved.

Lionel went close to her and threw his arms about her neck.

She started, as if she actually felt the contact, and sprang to her feet.

"Miss ——, Miss ——, don't you know me?" he cried; but while I could hear him, she evidently could not, though she looked about her in a half-frightened way.

Then, supposing that the touch and the presence she had felt were imaginary, she again fell upon her knees and went on with her interrupted prayer.

"Come away," I said to the boy; and we left her there with her dreams and her devotions.

That was the last I saw of Lionel. He bade me goodbye, saying:

"I shall stay near her for a few days. Perhaps I shall go back and forth, from her to you; but if I do not return, I will meet you again in a few years."

"Yes," I said, "it is affinity and desire which draw souls together, either on earth or in the other world."

When next I met the Teacher I told him about Lionel, and asked him if he thought the boy could come out to me now and then, after his life on earth had begun, as an unborn entity in the shelter of his mother's form.

"Probably not," he replied. "If he were an adept soul, he might do that; but with a soul of even high development, lacking real adeptship, it would be impossible."

"Yet," I said, "men living on earth do come out here in dreams."

"Yes, but when the soul enters matter, preparing for rebirth, it enters potentiality, if we may use the term, and all its strength is needed in the herculean effort to form the new body and adjust to it. After birth, when the eyes are opened, and the lungs are expanded to the air, the task is easier, and there may be left enough unused energy to bridge the gulf.

"But," he went on, "those who are soon to be mothers are often vaguely conscious of the souls they harbor. Even when they do not grasp the full significance of the miracle that is being performed through them, they have strange dreams and visions, which are mostly glimpses into the past incarnations of the unborn child. They see dream countries where the entity within has dwelt in the past; they feel desires which they cannot explain—reflected desires which are

•

merely the latent yearnings of the unborn one; they experience groundless fears which are its former dreads and terrors. The mother who nourishes a truly great soul, during this period of formation may herself grow spiritually beyond her own unaided possibility; while the mother of an unborn criminal often develops strange perversities, quite unlike her normal state of mind.

"If a woman were sufficiently intelligent and informed, she could judge from her own feelings and ideas what sort of soul was to be her child some day, and prepare to guide it accordingly. More knowledge is needed, here as elsewhere."

So, as in all my experiences, I learned something through the passing out of Lionel.

149

L E T T E R
34

THE BEAUTIFUL BEING

Yes, I have seen angels, if by angels you mean spiritual beings who have never dwelt as men upon the earth.

As a man is to a rock, so is an angel to a man in vividness of life. If we ever experienced that state of etheric joy, we have lost it through long association with matter. Can we ever regain it? Perhaps. The event is in our hand.

Shall I tell you of one whom I call the Beautiful Being? If it has a name in heaven, I have not heard it. Is the Beautiful Being man or woman? Sometimes it seems to be one, sometimes the other. There is a mystery here which I cannot fathom.

One night I seemed to be reclining upon a moonbeam, which means that the poet which dwells in all men was awake in me. I seemed to be reclining upon a moonbeam, and ecstasy filled my heart. For the moment I had escaped the clutches of Time, and was living in that etheric quietude which is merely the activity of rapture raised to the last degree. I must have been enjoying a foretaste of that paradoxical state which the wise ones of the East call Nirvana.

I was vividly conscious of the moonbeam and of myself, and *in* myself seemed to be everything else in the universe. It was the nearest I ever came to a realization of that supreme declaration, "*I am.*"

The past and the future seemed equally present in the moment. Had a voice whispered that it was yesterday, I should have acquiesced in the assertion; had I been told that it was a million years hence, I should have been also assentive. But whether it was really yesterday or a million years hence mattered not in the least. Perhaps the Beautiful Being only comes to those for whom the moment and eternity are one. I heard a voice say:

"Brother, it is I."

There was no question in my mind as to who had spoken. "It is I" can only be uttered in such a voice by one whose individuality is so vast as to be almost universal, one who has dipped in the ocean of the All, yet who knows the minute by reason of its own inclusiveness.

Standing before me was the Beautiful Being, radiant in its own light. Had it been less lovely I might have gasped with wonder; but the very perfection of its form and presence diffused an atmosphere of calm. I marveled not, because the state of my consciousness *was* marvel. I was lifted so far above the commonplace that I had no standard by which to measure the experience of that moment.

Imagine youth immortalized, the fleeting made eternal. Imagine the bloom of a child's face and the eyes of the ages of knowledge. Imagine the brilliancy of a thousand lives concentrated in those eyes, and the smile upon the lips of a love so pure that it asks no answering love from those it smiles upon.

But the language of earth cannot describe the unearthly, nor could the understanding of man grasp in a moment those joys which the Beautiful Being revealed to me in that hour of supreme life. For the possibilities of existence have been widened for me, the meanings of the soul have deepened. Those who behold the Beautiful Being are never the same again as they were before. They may forget for a time, and lose in the business of living the magic of that presence; but whenever they do remember, they are caught up again on the wings of the former rapture.

It may happen to one who is living upon the earth; it may happen to one in the spaces between the stars; but the experience must be the same when it comes to all; for only to one in the state in which *it* dwells could the Beautiful Being reveal itself at all.

A SONG OF THE BEAUTIFUL BEING

When you hear a rustling in the air, listen again: there may be something there.

When you feel a warmth mysterious and lovely in the heart, there may be something there, something sent to you from a warm and lovely source.

When a joy unknown fills your being, and your soul goes out, out . . . toward some loved mystery, you know not where, know that the mystery itself is reaching toward you with warm and loving, though invisible, arms.

We who live in the invisible are not invisible to each other.

There are tender colors here and exquisite forms, and the eye gloats on beauty never seen upon the earth.

Oh, the joy of simple life—to be, and to sing in your soul all day as the bird sings to its mate!

For you are singing to your mate whenever your soul sings.

Did you fancy it was only the springtime that thrilled you and moved you to listen to the rustling of wings?

153

The springtime of the heart is all time, and the autumn may never come.

Listen! When the lark sings, he sings to you. When the waters sing, they sing to you.

And as your heart rejoices, there is always another heart somewhere that responds; and the soul of the listening heavens grows glad with the mother joy.

I am glad to be here, I am glad to be there. There is beauty wherever I go.

Can you guess the reason, children of earth?

Come out and play with me in the daisy fields of space. I will wait for you at the corner where the four winds meet.

154

You will not lose your way, if you follow the gleam at the end of the garden of hope.

There is music also beyond the roar of the earth as it swishes through space:

There is music in keys unknown to the duller ears of the earth, and harmonies whose chords are souls attuned to each other.

Listen. . . . Do you hear them?

Oh, the ears are made for hearing, and the eyes are made for seeing, and the heart is made for loving!

The hours go by and leave no mark, and the years are as sylphs that dance on the air and leave no footprints, and the centuries march solemn and slow.

THE BEAUTIFUL BEING

But we smile, for joy is also in the solemn tread of the
centuries.

Joy, joy everywhere. It is for you and for me, and for
you as much as for me.

Will you meet me out where the four winds meet?

L E T T E R
35

THE HOLLOW SPHERE

Some time ago I started to write to you about certain visits which I had made to the infernal regions; but I was called away, and the letter was not finished. Tonight I will take up the story again.

You must know that there are many hells, and they are mostly of our own making. That is one of those platitudes which are based upon fact.

Desiring one day to see the particular kind of hell to which a drunkard would be likely to go, I sought that part of the hollow sphere around the world which corresponds to one of those countries where drunkenness is most common. Souls, when they come out, usually remain in the neighborhood where they have lived, unless there is some strong reason to the contrary.

I had no difficulty in finding a hell full of drunkards. What do you fancy they were doing? Repenting their sins? Not at all. They were hovering around those places on earth where the fumes of alcohol, and the heavier fumes of those who overindulge in alcohol, made sickening the atmosphere. It is no wonder that sensitive people dislike the neighborhood of drinking saloons.

You would draw back with disgust and refuse to write for me should I tell you all that I saw. One or two instances will suffice.

I placed myself in a sympathetic and neutral state, so that I could see into both worlds.

A young man with restless eyes and a troubled face entered one of those "gin palaces" in which gilding and highly polished imitation mahogany tend to impress the miserable wayfarer with the idea that he is enjoying the luxury of the "kingdoms of this world." The young man's clothes were threadbare, and his shoes had seen much wear. A stubble of beard was on his chin, for the price of a shave is the price of a drink, and a man takes that which he desires most—when he can get it.

He was leaning on the bar, drinking a glass of some soul-destroying compound. And close to him, taller than he and bending over him, with its repulsive, bloated, ghastly face pressed close to his, as if to smell his whiskey-tainted breath, was one of the most horrible astral beings which I have seen in this world since I came out. The hands of the creature (and I use that word to suggest its vitality)—the hands of the creature were clutching the young man's form, one long and naked arm was around his shoulders, the other around his hips. It was literally sucking the liquor-soaked life of its victim, absorbing him, using him, in the successful attempt to enjoy vicariously the passion which death had intensified.

But was that a creature in hell? you ask. Yes, for I could look into its mind and see its sufferings. For ever (the words "for ever" may be used of that which seems endless) this entity was doomed to crave and crave and never to be satisfied.

And the young man who leaned on the bar in that gilded palace of gin was filled with a nameless horror and sought to leave the place; but the arms of the thing that was now his master clutched him tighter and tighter, the sodden, vaporous cheek was pressed closer to his, the desire of the vampire creature aroused an answering desire in its victim, and the young man demanded another glass.

Verily, earth and hell are neighboring states, and the frontier has never been charted.

I have seen hells of lust and hells of hatred; hells of untruthfulness, where every object which the wretched dweller tried to grasp turned into something else which was a denial of the thing desired, where truth was mocked eternally and nothing was real, but everything—changing and uncertain as untruthfulness—became its own antithesis.

I have seen the anguished faces of those not yet resigned to lies, have seen their frantic efforts to clutch reality, which melted in their grasp. For the habit of untruthfulness, when carried into this world of shifting shapes, surrounds the untruthful person with ever-changing images which mock him and elude.

Beware of deathbed repentance and its after-harvest of morbid memories. It is better to go into eternity with one's karmic burdens bravely carried upon the back, rather than to slink through the back door of hell in the stockinged-feet of a sorry cowardice.

If you have sinned, accept the fact with courage and resolve to sin no more; but he who dwells upon his sins in his last hour will live them over and over again in the state beyond the tomb.

Every act is followed by its inevitable reaction; every cause is accompanied by its own effect, which nothing—save the powerful dynamics of Will itself—can modify; and when Will modifies the effect of an antecedent cause, it is always by setting up a counteracting and more powerful cause than the first—a cause so strong that the other is irresistibly carried along with it, as a great flood can sweep a trickling

stream of water from an open hose-pipe, carrying the hose-pipe cause and its trickling effect
along with the rushing torrent of its own flood.

If you recognize the fact that you have
sinned, set up good actions more powerful than
your sins, and reap the reward for those.

There is much more to be said about hells,
but this is enough for tonight. At another time
I may return to the subject.

L E T T E R

36

AN EMPTY CHINA CUP

It is no wonder that children, no matter how old and experienced their souls, have to be retaught in each life the relative values of all things according to the artificial standards of the world; for out here those values lose their meaning.

That a soul had houses, lands, and honors among men does not increase his value in our eyes. We cannot hope to profit by his discarded riches. The soul in the "hereafter" builds its own house, and the materials thereof are free as air. If I use the house which another has built, I miss the enjoyment of creating my own.

There is nothing worth stealing out here, so no one trembles for fear of burglars in the night. Even bores can be escaped by retiring to the very center of oneself, for a bore is himself too self-centered ever to pierce to the center of anyone else.

On earth you value titles, inherited or acquired; here a man's name is not of much

importance even to himself, and a visiting-card
would be lost through the cracks in the floor of
heaven. No footman angel would ever deliver it
to his Lord and Master.

One day I met a lady recently arrived. She
had not been here long enough to have lost her
assurance of superiority over ordinary men and
angels. That morning I had on my best Roman
toga, for I had been reliving the past; and the
lady, mistaking me for Caesar or some other
ancient aristocrat, asked me to direct her to a
place where gentlewomen congregated.

I was forced to admit that I did not know of
any such resort; but as the visitor seemed lonely
and bewildered, I invited her to rest beside me
for a time and to question me if she wished.

"I have been here several months," I said,
"and have gained considerable experience."

It was plain to see that she was puzzled by
my remark. She glanced at my classical garment,
and I could feel her thinking that there was
something incongruous between it and my assertion that I had been here only a few months.

"Perhaps you are an actor," she said.

"We are all actors here," I replied.

This seemed to puzzle her more than ever,
and she said that she did not understand. Poor
lady! I felt sorry for her, and I tried my best to
explain to her the conditions under which we live.

•

"You must know in the first place," I said, "that this is the land of realized ideals. Now a man who has always desired to be a king can play the part up here if he wishes to, and no one will laugh at him; for each spirit has some favorite dream which he acts out to his own satisfaction.

"We have, madam," I continued, "reacquired the tolerance and the courtesy of children who never ridicule one another's play."

"Is heaven merely a playroom?" she asked, in a shocked tone.

"Not at all," I answered; "but you are not in heaven."

Her look of apprehension caused me immediately to add:

"Nor are you in hell, either. What was your religion upon the earth?"

"Why, I professed the usual religion of my country and station; but I never gave it much thought."

"Perhaps the idea of purgatory is not unfamiliar to you."

"I am not a papist," she said, with some warmth.

"Nevertheless, a papist in your position would conceive himself to be in purgatory."

"I am certainly not happy," she admitted, "because everything is so strange."

"Have you no friends here?" I inquired.

"I must have many acquaintances," she said; "but I never cared for intimate friendships. I used to entertain a good deal; my husband's political position demanded it."

"Perhaps there is someone on this side to whom you were specially kind at some time or other, someone whose grief you helped to bear, whose poverty you eased."

"I patronized our religious charities."

"I fear that sort of help is too impersonal to be remembered here. Have you no children?"

"No."

"No brothers or sisters on this side?"

"I quarreled with my only brother for marrying beneath him."

"But surely," I said, "you must have had a mother. Was she not waiting for you when you came over?"

"No."

This surprised me, for I had been told that all mother spirits who have not gone back to the world know by a peculiar thrill when a child to which they have given birth is about to be reborn into the spiritual world—a sort of sympathetic after-pain, the final and sweetest reward of motherhood.

"Then she must have reincarnated," I said.

"Do you hold to that pagan belief?" the lady inquired, with just a touch of superiority.

•

"I thought that only queer people, Theosophists and such, believed in reincarnation."

"I was always queer," I admitted. "But you know, of course, dear madam, that about three-quarters of the earth's inhabitants are familiar with that theory in some form or other."

We continued our talk for a little time, and meanwhile I was puzzling my heart as to what I could do to help this poor lonely woman, for whom no one was waiting. I passed in mental review this and that ministering angel of my acquaintance, and wondered which of them would be considered most correct from the conventional earthly point of view. The noblest of them was usually at the side of some newly arrived unfortunate woman—to use a euphemism of that polite society which my latest *protégée* had frequented. The others were here, there, and everywhere, but generally with those souls who needed them most; while the need of my present companion was more real than urgent. If Lionel had been here, he might have entertained her for a while.

I wished that I had cultivated the acquaintance of some of those ladies who crochet and gossip in this world as they crocheted and gossiped in yours. Do not be shocked. Did you fancy that a lifelong habit could be laid aside in a moment? As women on earth dream often of their knitting, so they do here. It is as easy to knit in this world as it is to dream in yours.

Understand that the world in which I now live is no more essentially sacred than is the world in which you live, nor is it any more mysterious to those who dwell in it. To the serious soul all conditions are sacred—except those that are profane, and both are found out here as well as on the earth.

But to return to the lonely woman. I was still wondering what I should do with her when, looking up, I saw the Teacher approaching. He had with him another woman, as like the first as one empty china cup is like another empty china cup. Then he and I went away and left the two together.

"I did not know," I said to the Teacher, "that you troubled yourself with any souls but those of considerable development."

He smiled:

"It was your perplexity which I came to relieve, not that of those poor ladies."

Then he began to talk to me about relative values.

"In a sense," he said, "one soul is as much worth helping as another; in a deeper sense, perhaps it is not. Do not think that I am indifferent to the sufferings of the weakest ones because I give my time and attention to the strong. Like the ministering angels, I go where I am most needed. Only the strong ones can learn what I have to teach. The weak ones are the charges of the Messiahs and their followers. But, nevertheless, between us and the Messiahs there is brotherhood and there is mutual understanding. Each works in his own field. The Messiahs help the many; we help the few. Their reward in love is greater than ours; but we do not work for reward any more than they do. Each follows the law of his being.

"To be loved by all men a teacher must be known to all men, and we reveal ourselves only to a few chosen ones. Why do we not go the way of the Messiahs? Because the balance must be maintained. For every great worker in the sight of men there is another worker out of sight. Which kind of teacher is of greater value? The question is out of order. The North and the South are interdependent, and there are two poles to every magnet."

•

LETTER

37

WHERE TIME IS NOT

I think you now understand from what I have said that not all the souls who have passed the airy frontier are either in heaven or hell. Few reach an extreme, and most live out their allotted period here as they lived out their allotted period on earth, without realizing either the possibilities or the significance of their condition.

Wisdom is a tree of slow growth; the rings around its trunk are earthly lives, and the grooves between are the periods between the lives. Who grieves that an acorn is slow in becoming an oak? It is equally unphilosophical to feel that the truth which I have endeavored to make you understand—the truth of the soul's great leisure—is necessarily sad. If a man were to become an archangel in a few years' time, he would suffer terribly from growing pains. The Law is implacable, but it often seems to be kind.

•

Nevertheless, there are many souls in heaven, and there are many heavens, of which I have seen a few.

But do not fancy that most people go from place to place and from state to state as I do. The things which I describe to you are not exceptional; but that one man should be able to see and describe so many things is exceptional indeed. I owe it largely to the Teacher. Without his guidance I could not have acquired so rich an experience.

Yes, there are many heavens. Last night I felt the yearning for beauty which sometimes came to me on earth. One of the strangest phenomena of this ethereal world is the tremendous attraction by sympathy—the attraction of events, I mean. Desire a thing intensely enough, and you are on the way to it. A body of a feather's weight moves swiftly when propelled by a free will.

I felt a yearning for beauty, which is a synonym for heaven. Did I really move from my place, or did heaven come to me? I cannot say; *space means so little here.* For every vale without there is a vale within. We desire a place, and we are there. Perhaps the Teacher could give you a scientific explanation of this, but I cannot at the moment. And then, I want to tell you about that heaven where I was last night. It was so beautiful that the charm of it is over me still.

•

I saw a double row of dark-topped trees, like cypresses, and at the end of this long avenue down which I passed was a softly diffused light. Somewhere I have read of a heaven lighted by a thousand suns, but my heaven was not like that. The light as I approached it was softer than moonlight, though clearer. Perhaps the light of the sun would shine as softly if seen through many veils of alabaster. Yet this light seemed to come from nowhere. It simply was.

As I approached I saw two beings walking towards me, hand in hand. There was such a look of happiness on their faces as one never sees on the faces of earth. Only a spirit unconscious of time could look like that.

170

I should say that these two were man and woman, save that they seemed so different from what you understand by man and woman. They did not even look at each other as they walked; the touch of the hand seemed to make them so much one, that the realization of the eye could have added nothing to their content. Like the light which came from nowhere, they simply were.

A little farther on I saw a group of bright-robed children dancing among flowers. Hand in hand in a ring they danced, and their garments, which were like the petals of flowers, moved with the rhythm of their dancing limbs. A great

•

joy filled my heart. They, too, were unconscious of time, and might have been dancing there from eternity, for all I knew. But whether their gladness was of the moment or of the ages had no significance for me or for them. Like the light, and like the lovers who had passed me hand in hand, they were, and that was enough.

I had left the avenue of cypresses and stood in a wide plain, encircled by a forest of blossoming trees. The odors of spring were on the air, and the birds sang. In the center of the plain a great circular fountain played with the waters, tossing them in the air, whence they descended in feathery spray. An atmosphere of inexpressible charm was over everything. Here and there in this circular flower-scented heaven walked angelic beings, many or most of whom must some time have been human. Two by two they walked, or in groups, smiling to themselves or at one another.

On earth you often use the word "peace"; but compared with the peace of that place, the greatest peace of earth is only turmoil. I realized that I was in one of the fairest heavens, but that I was alone there.

No sooner had this thought of solitude found lodgment in my heart than I saw standing before me the Beautiful Being about whom I wrote you a little time ago. It smiled, and said to me:

171

●

"He who is sadly conscious of his solitude is no longer in heaven. So I have come to hold you here yet a little while."

"Is this the particular heaven where you dwell?" I asked.

"Oh, I dwell nowhere and everywhere," the Beautiful Being answered. "I am one of the voluntary wanderers, who find the charm of home in every heavenly or earthly place."

"So you sometimes visit earth?"

"Yes, even the remotest hells I go to, but I never stay there long. My purpose is to know all things, and yet to remain unattached."

"And do you love the earth?"

172

"The earth is one of my playgrounds. I sing to the children of earth sometimes; and when I sing to the poets, they believe that their muse is with them. Here is a song which I sang one night to a soul which dwells among men:"

My sister, I am often with you when you realize it not.

For me a poet soul is a well of water in whose deeps I can see myself reflected.

I live in a glamour of light and color, which you mortal poets vainly try to express in magic words.

I am in the sunset and in the stars; I watched the moon grow old and you grow young.

•

WHERE TIME IS NOT

In childhood you sought for me in the swiftly moving clouds; in maturity you fancied you had caught me in the gleam of a lover's eye; but I am the eluder of men.

I beckon and I fly, and the touch of my feet does not press down the heads of the blossoming daisies.

You can find me and lose me again, for mortal cannot hold me.

I am nearest to those who seek beauty—whether in thought or in form; I fly from those who seek to imprison me.

You can come each day to the region where I dwell.

Sometimes you will meet me, sometimes not; for my will is the wind's will, and I answer no beckoning finger:

But when I beckon, the souls come flying from the four corners of heaven.

Your soul comes flying, too; for you are one of those I have called by the spell of my magic.

I have use for you, and you have meaning for me; I like to see your soul in its hours of dream and ecstasy.

Whenever one of my own dreams a dream of Paradise, the light grows brighter for me, to whom all things are bright.

Oh, forget not the charm of the moment, forget not
the lure of the mood!

For the mood is wiser than all the magi of earth, and
the treasures of the moment are richer and rarer
than the hoarded wealth of the ages.

The moment is real, while the age is only a delusion,
a memory, and a shadow.

Be sure that each moment is all, and the moment is
more than time.

Time carries an hourglass, and his step is slow; his
hair is white with the rime of years, and his scythe
is dull with unwearied mowing;

But he never yet has caught the moment in its flight.
He has grown old in casting nets for it.

Ah, the magic of life and of the endless combinations
of living things!

I was young when the sun was formed, and I shall be
young when the moon falls dead in the arms of
her daughter the earth.

Will you not be young with me? The dust is as nothing: the soul is all.

Like a crescent moon on the surface of a lake of water
is the moment of love's awakening;

Like a faded flower in the lap of the tired world is the
moment of love's death.

But there is love and Love, and the love of the light
  for its radiance is the love of souls for each other.

There is no death where the inner light shines, irradi-
  ating the fields of the within—the beyond—the
  unattainable attainment.

You know where to find me.

175

L E T T E R
38

THE DOCTRINE OF DEATH

Many times during the months in which I have been here have I seen men and women lying in a state of unconsciousness more profound than the deepest sleep, their faces expressionless and uninteresting. At first, before I understood the nature of their sleep, I tried as an experiment to awaken one or two of them, and was not successful. In certain cases where my curiosity was aroused, I have returned later, day after day, and found them still lying in the same lethargy.

"Why," I asked myself, "should any man sleep like that—a sleep so deep that neither the spoken word nor the physical touch could arouse him?"

One day when the Teacher was with me we passed one of those unconscious men whom I had seen before, had watched, and had striven unsuccessfully to arouse.

"Who are these people who sleep like that?" I asked the Teacher; and he replied:

"They are those who in their earth life denied the immortality of the soul after death."

"How terrible!" I said. "And will they never awaken?"

"Yes, perhaps centuries, perhaps ages hence, when the irresistible law of rhythm shall draw them out of their sleep into incarnation. For the law of rebirth is one with the law of rhythm."

"Would it not be possible to awaken one of them, this man, for instance?"

"You have attempted it, have you not?" the Teacher inquired, with a keen look into my face.

"Yes," I admitted.

"And you failed?"

"Yes."

We looked at each other for a moment, then I said:

"Perhaps you, with your greater power and knowledge, could succeed where I have failed."

He made no answer. His silence fired my interest still further, and I said eagerly:

"Will you not try? Will you not awaken this man?"

"You know not what you ask," he replied.

"But tell me this," I demanded: "could you awaken him?"

"Perhaps. But in order to counteract the law which holds him in sleep, the law of the spell he laid upon his own soul when he went out of life

demanding unconsciousness and annihilation—
in order to counteract that law, I should have to
put in operation a law still stronger."

"And that is?" I asked.

"Will," he answered, "the potency of will."

"Could you?"

"As I said before—perhaps."

"And will you?"

"Again I say that you know not what you ask."

"Will you please explain?" I persisted, "for
indeed this seems to me to be one of the most
marvelous things which I have seen."

The face of the Teacher was very grave, as he
answered:

"What good has this man done in the past
that I should place myself between him and the
law of cause and effect which he has willfully set
in operation?"

"I do not know his past," I said.

"Then," the Teacher demanded, "will you tell
me your reason for asking me to do this thing?"

"My reason?"

"Yes. Is it pity for this man's unfortunate condition, or is it scientific curiosity on your part?"

I should gladly have been able to say that it
was pity for the man's sad state which moved me
so; but one does not juggle with truth or with
motives when speaking to such a Teacher, so I
admitted that it was scientific curiosity.

•

"In that case," he said, "I am justified in using him as a demonstration of the power of the trained will."

"It will not harm him, will it?"

"On the contrary. And though he may suffer shock, it will probably be the means of so impressing his mind that never again, even in future lives on earth, can he believe himself, or teach others to believe, that death ends everything. As far as he is concerned, he does not deserve that I should waste upon him so great an amount of energy as will be necessary to arouse him from this sleep, this spell which he laid upon himself ages ago. But if I awaken him, it will be for your sake, 'that you may believe.'"

I wish I could describe the scene which took place, so that you could see it with the eyes of your imagination. There lay the man at our feet, his face colorless and expressionless, and above him towered the splendid form of the Teacher, his face beautiful with power, his eyes brilliant with thought.

"Can you not see," asked the Teacher, "a faint light surrounding this seemingly lifeless figure?"

"Yes, but the light is very faint indeed."

"Nevertheless," said the Teacher, "that light is far less faint than is this weak soul's hold upon the eternal truth. But where you see only a pale light around the recumbent form, I see in that

•

light many pictures of the soul's past. I see that
he not only denied immortality of the soul's consciousness, but that he taught his doctrine of
death to other men and made them even as himself. Truly he does not deserve that I should try
to awaken him!"

"Yet you will do it?"

"Yes, I will do it."

I regret that I am not permitted to tell you
by what form of words and by what acts
my Teacher succeeded, after a mighty effort,
in arousing that man from his self-imposed imitation of annihilation. I realized as never
before—not only the personal power of my
Teacher, but the irresistible power of a trained
and directed will.

I thought of that scene recorded in the New
Testament, where Jesus said to the dead man in
the tomb, "Lazarus, come forth!"

"The soul of man is immortal," declared
the Teacher, looking fixedly into the shrinking
eyes of the awakened man and holding them by
his will.

"The soul of man is immortal," he repeated.
Then in a tone of command:

"Stand up!"

The man struggled to his feet. Though
his body was light as a feather, as are all our
bodies here, I could see that his slumbering

180

•

energy was still almost too dormant to permit of that really slight exertion.

"You live," declared the Teacher. "You have passed through death, and you live. Do not dare to deny that you live. You cannot deny it."

"But I do not believe ——" began the man, his stubborn materialism still challenging the truth of his own existence, his memory surviving the ordeal through which he had passed. This last surprised me more than anything else. But after a moment's stupefaction, I understood that it was the power of the Teacher's mental picture of the astral records round this soul which had forced those memories to awaken.

"Sit down between us two," said the Teacher to the newly aroused man, "and let us reason together. You thought yourself a great reasoner, did you not, when you walked the earth as So-and so?"

"I did."

"You see that you were mistaken in your reasoning," the Teacher went on, "for you certainly passed through death, and you are now alive."

"But where am I?" He looked about him in a bewildered way. "Where am I, and who are you?"

"You are in eternity," replied the Teacher, "where you always have been and always will be."

"And you?"

"I am one who knows the workings of the Law."

"What law?"

"The law of rhythm, which drives the soul into and out of gross matter, as it drives the tides of the ocean into flood and ebb, and the consciousness of man into sleeping and waking."

"And it was you who awakened me? Are you, then, this law of rhythm?"

The Teacher smiled.

"I am not the law," he said, "but I am bound by it, even as you, save as I am temporarily able to transcend it by my will—again, even as you."

I caught my breath at the profundity of this simple answer, but the man seemed not to observe its significance. Even as he! Why, this man by his misdirected will had been able temporarily to transcend the law of immortality, even as the Teacher by his wisely directed will transcended the mortal in himself! My soul sang within me at this glimpse of the godlike possibilities of the human mind.

"How long have I been asleep?" demanded the man.

"In what year did you die?" the Teacher asked.

"In the year 1817."

"And the present year is known, according to the Christian calendar, as the year 1912. You have lain in a death-like sleep for ninety-five years."

"And was it really you who awakened me?"

"Yes."

"Why did you do it?"

"Because it suited my good pleasure," was the Teacher's rather stern reply. "It was not because you deserved to be awakened."

"And how long would I have slept if you had not aroused me?"

"I cannot say. Probably until those who had started even with you had left you far behind on the road of evolving life. Perhaps for centuries, perhaps for ages."

"You have taken a responsibility upon yourself," said the man.

183

"You do not need to remind me of that," replied the Teacher. "I weighed in my own mind the full responsibility and decided to assume it for a purpose of my own. For will is free."

"Yet you overpowered my will."

"I did; but by my own more potent will, more potent because wisely directed and backed by a greater energy."

"And what are you going to do with me?"

"I am going to assume the responsibility of your training."

"My training?"

"Yes."

"And you will make things easy for me?"

"On the contrary, I shall make things very hard for you; but you cannot escape my teaching."

"Shall you instruct me personally?"

"Personally in the sense that I shall place you under the instruction of an advanced pupil of my own."

"Who? This man here?" He pointed to me.

"No. He is better occupied. I will take you to your teacher presently."

"And what will he show me?"

"The panorama of immortality. And when you have learned the lesson so that you can never forget nor escape it, you will have to go back to the earth and teach it to others; you will have to convert as many men to the truth of immortality as you have in the past deluded and misled by your false doctrines of materialism and death."

"And what if I refuse? You have said that will is free."

"*Do* you refuse?"

"No, but what if I had?

"Then, instead of growing and developing under the law of action and reaction, which in the East they call karma, you would have been its victim."

"I do not understand you."

"He is indeed a wise man," said the Teacher, "who understands the law of karma, which is also the law of cause and effect. But come. I will now take you to your new instructor."

Then, leaving me alone, the Teacher and his charge disappeared in the gray distance.

I remained there a long time, pondering what I had seen and heard.

L E T T E R

39

The Celestial Hierarchy

I am about to say something which may shock certain persons; but those who are too fond of their own ideas, without being willing to grant others their ideas in turn, should not seek to open the jealously guarded doors which separate the land of the so-called living from the land of the certainly not dead.

This is the statement which I have to make: that there are many gods, and that the One God is the sum total of all of them. All gods exist in God. Do what you like with that statement, dear world, for truth is more vital than anybody's dream, even yours or mine.

Have I seen God? I have seen Him who has been called the Son of God, and you may remember that He said that whoever had seen the Son had seen the Father.

But what of the other gods? you ask; for there are many in the world's pantheons. Well, the realities exist out here.

•

What! you say again, can man create the gods
of his imagination and give them a place in the
invisible? No. They existed here first, and man
became aware of them long ago through his own
psychic and spiritual perception of them. Man did
not create them, and the materialists who say that
he did know little of the laws of being. Man,
primitive man, perceived them through his own
spiritual affinities with and nearness to them.

When you have read folktales of this god and
that, you have perhaps spoken patronizingly of
the old myth-makers and thanked your lucky
stars that you lived in a more enlightened age.
But those old storytellers were the really enlightened ones, for they saw into the other world and
recorded what they saw.

Many of the world's favorite gods are said to
have lived upon the earth as men. They have so
lived. Does that idea startle you?

How does a man become a god, and how
does a god become a man? Have you ever wondered? A man becomes a god by developing
god-consciousness, which is not the same as
developing his own thought *about* God. During
recent years you have heard and read much of
so-called Masters, men of superhuman attain-
ments, who have forgone the small pleasures
and recognitions of the world in order to achieve
something greater.

Man's ideas of the gods change as the gods themselves change, for "everything is becoming," as Heraclitus said about twenty-four centuries ago. Did you fancy that the gods stood still, and that only you progressed? In that case you might someday outstrip your god, and fall to worshiping yourself, having nothing to look up to as superior.

Accompanied by the Teacher, I have stood face to face with some of the older gods. Had I come out here with a superior contempt for all gods save my own, I should hardly have been granted that privilege; for the gods are as exclusive as they are inclusive, and they only reveal themselves to those who can see them as they are.

Does this open the door to polytheism, pantheism, or other dreaded *isms*? An *ism* is only a word. Facts are. The day is past when men were burned at the stake for having had a vision of the wrong god. But even now I would hesitate to tell all that I have learned about the gods, though I can tell you much.

Take, for instance, the god whom the Romans called Neptune. Did you fancy that he was only a poetic creation of the old mythmakers? He was something more than that. He was supposed to rule the ocean. Now, what could be more orderly and inevitable than that the work of controlling the elements and the floods should be assumed by, and the work parceled out among, those able to perform it? We hear much of the laws of Nature. Who enforces them? The term "natural law" is in every man's mouth, but the Law has executors in heaven as on earth.

I have been told that there are also planetary beings, planetary gods, though I have never had the honor of conscious communion with one of them. If a planetary being is so far beyond the daring of my approach, how should I comport myself in approaching the God of gods?

O paradoxical mind of man, which stands in awe and trembling before the servant, yet approaches the master without fear!

I have been told that the guardian spirit of this planet Earth evolved himself into a god of tremendous power and responsibility in bygone cycles of existence. To him who has ever used a microscope, the idea need not be appalling. The infinitely small and the infinitely great are the tail and the head of the Eternal Serpent.

Who do you fancy will be the gods of the future cycles of existence? Will they not be those who in this cycle of planetary life have raised themselves above the mortal? Will they not be the strongest and the most sublime among the present spirits of men? Even the gods must have their resting period, and those in office now would doubtless wish to be supplanted.

To those men who are ambitious for growth, the doors of development are always open.

L E T T E R
40

THE DARLING OF THE UNSEEN

I have written you before of one whom I call the Beautiful Being, one whose province seems to be the universe, whose chosen companions are all men and angelkind, whose playthings are days and ages.

For some reason, the Beautiful Being has lately been so gracious as to take an interest in my efforts to acquire knowledge, and has shown me many things which otherwise I should never have seen.

When a tour of the planet is personally conducted by an angel, the traveler is specially favored. Letters of introduction to the great and powerful of earth are nothing compared with this introduction, for by its means I see into the souls of all beings, and my visits to their houses are not limited to the drawing rooms. The Beautiful Being has access everywhere.

Did you ever fancy when you had had a lovely dream that maybe an angel had kissed you in your sleep? I have seen such things.

•

Oh, do not be afraid of giving rein to your imagination! It is the wonderful things which are really true; the commonplace things are nearly all false. When a great thought lifts you by the hair, do not cling hold of the solid earth. Let go. He whom an inspiration seizes might even—if he dared to trust his vision—behold the Beautiful Being face to face, as I have. When flying through the air, one's sight is keen. If one goes fast and high enough, one may behold the inconceivable.

The other night I was meditating on a flower seed, for there is nothing so small that it may not contain a world. I was meditating on a flower seed, and amusing myself by tracing its history, generation by generation, back to the dawn of time. I smile as I use that figure, "the dawn of time," for time has had so many dawns and so many sunsets, and still it is unwearied.

I had traced the genealogy of the seed back to the time when the caveman forgot his fighting in the strangely disturbing pleasure of smelling the fragrance of its parent flower, when I heard a low musical laugh in my left ear, and something as light as a butterfly's wing brushed my cheek on that side.

I turned to look, and quick as a flash, I heard the laughter in the other ear, while another butter-fly touch came on my right cheek. Then some-

192

thing like a veil was blown across my eyes, and a clear voice said:

"Guess who it is!"

I was all a-thrill with the pleasure of this divine play, and I answered:

"Perhaps you are the fairy that makes blind children dream of daisy fields."

"However did you know me?" laughed the Beautiful Being, unwinding the veil from my eyes. "I am indeed that fairy. But you must have been peeping through cracks in the door when I touched the eyes of the blind babies."

"I am always peeping through cracks in the door of the earth people's chamber," I replied.

The Beautiful Being laughed again:

"Will you come and have another peep with me this evening?"

"With pleasure."

"You could not do it with pain if I were by," was the response.

And we started then and there upon the strangest evening's round which I have ever made.

We began by going to the house of a friend of mine and standing quietly in the room where he and his family were at supper. No one saw us but the cat, which began a loud purring and stretched itself with joy at our presence. Had I gone there alone, the cat might have been afraid of me; but who—even a cat—could fear the Beautiful Being?

Suddenly one of the children—the youngest one—looked up from his supper of bread and milk, and said:

"Father, why does milk taste good?"

"I really do not know," admitted the author of his being, "perhaps because the cow enjoyed giving it."

"That father might have been a poet," the Beautiful Being said to me; but no one overheard the remark.

One of the other children complained of feeling sleepy, and put his head down on the edge of the table. The mother started to arouse him, but the Beautiful Being fluttered a mystifying veil before her eyes, and she could not do it.

"Let him sleep if he wants to," she said. "I will put him to bed by and by."

I could see in the brain of the child that he was dreaming already, and I knew that the Beautiful Being was weaving a fairy tale on the web of his mind. After only a moment he started up, wide awake.

"I dreamed," he said, "that —— [the writer of these letters] was standing over there and smiling at me as he used to smile, and with him was an angel. I never saw an angel before."

•

"Come away," whispered the Beautiful Being to me. "From dreaming children nothing can be hidden."

We then paid a visit to the future mother of my boy Lionel. Oh, mystery of maternity! The eyes of the Beautiful Being were like stars as we gazed upon this other flower seed, whose genealogy goes even beyond the days of the caveman—aye, back to the time of the fire-mist and the sons of the morning stars.

"Come away!" said the Beautiful Being again. "To brides who dream of motherhood much also is revealed, and for this evening we remain unknown."

We passed along the margin of a river which divides a busy town. Suddenly from a house by the riverbank we heard the tinkle of a guitar and a woman's sweet voice singing:

195

> When other lips and other hearts
> Their tale of love shall tell, . . .
> Then you'll remember—you'll remember me.

The Beautiful Being touched my hand and whispered:

"The life that is so sweet to these mortals is a book of enchantment for me."

"Yet you have never tasted human life yourself?"

•

"On the contrary, I taste it every day; but I only taste it—and pass on. Should I consume it, I might not be able to pass on."

"But do you never long so to consume it?"

"Oh, but the thrill is in the taste! Digestion is a more or less tiresome process."

"I fear you are a divine wanton," I said, affectionately.

"Be careful," answered the Beautiful Being. "He who fears anything will lose me in the fog of his own fears."

"You irresistible one!" I cried. "Who are you? *What* are you?"

"Did you not say yourself a little while ago that I was the fairy who made blind babies dream of daisy fields?"

"I love you," I said, "with an incomprehensible love."

"All love is incomprehensible," the Beautiful Being answered. "But come, brother, let us climb the hill of vision. When you are out of breath, if you catch at my flying veil I will wait till you are rested."

Strange things we saw that night. I should weary you if I told you all of them.

We stood on the crater of an active volcano and watched the dance of the fire-spirits. Did you fancy that salamanders were only seen by unabstemious poets? They are as real—to themselves and to those who see them—as are the omnibus drivers in the streets of London.

The real and the unreal! If I were writing an essay now, instead of the narrative of a traveler in a strange country, I should have much to say on the subject of the real and the unreal.

The Beautiful Being has changed my ideas about the whole universe. I wonder if, when I come back to the earth again, I shall remember all the marvels I have seen. Perhaps, like most people, I shall have forgotten the details of my life before birth, and shall bring with me only vague yearnings after the inexpressible, and the deep unalterable conviction that there are more things in earth and heaven than are dreamed of in the philosophy of the world's people. Perhaps if I almost remember, but not quite, I shall be a poet in my next life. Worse things might happen to me.

What an adventure it is, this launching of one's bark upon the sea of rebirth!

But by my digressions one would say that I was in my second childhood. So I am—my second childhood in the so-called invisible.

When, on my voyage that night with the Beautiful Being, I had feasted my eyes upon beauty until they were weary, my companion led me to scenes on the earth which, had I beheld them alone, would have made me very sad.

•

But no one can be sad when the Beautiful Being is near. That is the charm of that marvelous entity; to be in its presence is to taste the joys of immortal life.

We looked on at a midnight revel in what you on earth would call "a haunt of vice." Was I shocked and horrified? Not at all. I watched the antics of those human animalcula as a scientist might watch the motions of the smaller living creatures in a drop of water. It seemed to me that I saw it all from the viewpoint of the stars. I started to say from the viewpoint of God, to whom small and great are the same; but perhaps the stellar simile is the truer one, for how can we judge of what God sees—unless we mean the god in us?

You who read what I have written, perhaps when you come out here you will have many surprises. The small things may seem larger and the large things smaller, and everything may take its proper place in the infinite plan, of which even your troubles and perplexities are parts, inevitable and beautiful.

That idea came to me as I wandered from heaven to earth, from beauty to ugliness, with my angelic companion.

I wish I could explain the influence of the Beautiful Being. It is unlike anything else in the universe. It is elusive as a moonbeam, yet more

sympathetic than a mother. It is daintier than a
rose, yet it looks upon ugly things with a smile.
It is purer than the breath of the sea, yet it seems
to have no horror of impurity. It is artless as a
child, yet wiser than the ancient gods, a marvel
of paradoxes, a celestial vagabond, the darling of
the unseen.

•

L E T T E R

4I

A Victim of the Nonexistent

The other day I met an acquaintance, a woman whom I had known for a number of years, and who came out about the time I did.

Old acquaintances when they meet here greet each other about as they did on earth. Though we are, as a rule, less conventional than you, still we cling more or less to our former habits.

I asked Mrs. —— how she was enjoying herself, and she said that she was not having a very pleasant time. She found that everybody was interested in something else, and did not want to talk with her.

This was the first time I had met with such a complaint, and I was struck by its peculiarity. I asked her to what cause she attributed this unsociability, and she replied that she did not know the cause, that it had puzzled her.

"What do you talk to them about?" I asked.

•

"Why, I tell them my troubles, as one friend tells another; but they do not seem to be interested. How selfish people are!"

Poor soul! She did not realize here, any more than she had on earth, that our troubles are not interesting to anybody but ourselves.

"Suppose," I said, "that you unburden yourself to me. Tell me your troubles. I will promise not to run away."

"Why, I hardly know where to begin!" she answered. "I have found so many unpleasant things."

"What, for instance?"

"Why, horrid people. I remember that when I lived in ——, I sometimes told myself that in the other world I would not be bothered with boardinghouse landladies and their careless hired girls; but they are just as bad here—even worse."

"Do you mean to tell me that you live in a boardinghouse here?"

"Where should I live? You know that I am not rich."

Of all the astonishing things I had heard in this land of changes, this was the most astonishing. A boardinghouse in the "invisible" world! Surely, I told myself, my observations had been limited. Here was a new discovery.

•

"Is the table good in your boardinghouse?" I asked.

"No, it is worse than at the last one."

"Are the meals scanty?"

"Yes, scanty and bad, especially the coffee."

"Will you tell me," I said, my wonder growing, "if you really eat three meals a day here, as you used to do on earth?"

"How strangely you talk!" she answered, in a sharp tone. "I don't find very much difference between this place and the earth, as you call it, except that I am more uncomfortable here, because everything is so flighty and uncertain."

"Yes, go on."

"I never know in the morning who will be sitting next me in the evening. They come and go."

"And what do you eat?"

"The same old things—meat and potatoes, and pies and puddings."

"And you still eat these things?"

"Why, yes; don't you?"

I hardly knew how to reply. Had I told her what my life here really was, she would no more have understood than she would have understood two years ago, when we lived in the same city on earth, had I told her then what my real mental life was. So I said:

"I have not much appetite."

She looked at me as if she distrusted me in some way, though why I could not say.

"Are you still interested in philosophy?" she asked.

"Yes. Perhaps that is why I don't get hungry very often."

"You were always a strange man."

"I suppose so. But tell me, Mrs. ——, do you never feel a desire to leave all this behind?"

"To leave all what behind?"

"Why, boardinghouses and uncongenial people, and meat and potatoes, and pies and puddings, and the shadows of material things in general."

"What do you mean by 'the *shadows* of material things'?"

"I mean that these viands and pastries, which you eat and do not enjoy, are not real. They have no real existence."

"Why!" she exclaimed, "have you become a Christian Scientist?"

At this I laughed heartily. Was one who denied the reality of astral food in the astral world a Christian Scientist, because the Christian Scientists denied the reality of material food in the material world? The analogy tickled my fancy.

"Let me convert you to Christian Science, then," I said.

"No, sir!" was her sharp response. "You never

succeeded in convincing me that there was any truth in your various fads and philosophies. And now you tell me that the food I eat is not real."

I puzzled for a moment, trying to find a way by which the actual facts of her condition could be brought home to the mind of this poor woman. Finally I hit upon the right track.

"Do you realize," I said, "that you are only dreaming?"

"What!" she snapped at me.

"Yes, you are dreaming. All this is a dream—these boardinghouses, *et cetera*."

"If that is so, perhaps you would like to wake me up."

"I certainly should. But you will have to awaken yourself, I fancy. Tell me, what were your ideas about the future life, before you came out here?"

"What do you mean by *out here*?"

"Why, before you died?"

"But, man, I am not dead!"

"Of course you are not dead. Nobody is dead. But you certainly understand that you have changed your condition."

"Yes, I have noticed a change, and a change for the worse."

"Don't you remember your last illness?"

"Yes."

"And that you passed out?"

"Yes, if you call it that."

"You know that you have left your body?"

She looked down at her form, which appeared as usual, even to its rusty black dress rather out of date.

"But I still have my body," she said.

"Then you have not missed the other one?"

"No."

"And you don't know where it is?"

My amazement was growing deeper and deeper. Here was a phenomenon I had not met before.

"I suppose," she said, "that they must have buried my body, if you say I left it; but this one is just the same to me."

"Has it always seemed the same?" I asked, remembering my own experiences when I first came out, my difficulty in adjusting the amount of energy I used to the lightness of my new body.

"Now you mention it," she said, "I do recall having some trouble a year or two ago. I was quite confused for a long time. I think I must have been delirious."

"Yes, doubtless you were," I answered. "But tell me, Mrs. ——, have you no desire to visit heaven?"

"Why, I always supposed that I should visit heaven when I died; but, as you see, I am not dead."

•

"Still," I said, "I can take you to heaven now, perhaps, if you would like to go."

"Are you joking?"

"Not at all. Will you come?"

"Are you certain that I can go there without dying?"

"But I assure you *there are no dead.*"

As we went slowly along, for I thought it best not to hurry her too swiftly from one condition to another, I drew a word-picture of the place we were about to visit—the orthodox Christian heaven. I described the happy and loving people who stood in the presence of their Savior, in the soft radiance from the central Light.

"Perhaps," I said, "some dwellers in that country see the face of God Himself, as they expected to see it when they were on earth; as for myself, I saw only the Light, and afterwards the figure of the Christ."

"I have often wished to see Christ," said my companion in an awestruck voice. "Do you think that I can really see Him?"

"I think so, if you believe strongly that you will."

"And what were they doing in heaven when you were there?" she asked.

"They were worshiping God, and they were happy."

"I want to be happy," she said; "I have never been very happy."

"The great thing in heaven," I advised, "is to love all the others. That is what makes them happy. If they loved the face of God only, it would not be quite heaven; for the joy of God is the joy of union."

Thus, by subtle stages, I led her mind away from astral boardinghouses to the ideas of the orthodox spiritual world, which was probably the only spiritual world which she could understand.

I spoke of the music—yes, church music, if you like to call it that. I created in her wandering and chaotic mind a fixed desire for sabbath joys and sabbath peace, and the communion of friends in heaven. But for this gradual preparation she could not have adjusted herself to the conditions of that world.

When we stood in the presence of those who worship God with song and praise, she seemed caught up on a wave of enthusiasm, to feel that at last she had come home.

I wanted to take leave of her in such a way that she would not come out again to look for me; so I held out my hand in the old way and said good-bye, promising to come again and visit her there, and advising her to stay where she was. I think she will. Heaven has a strong hold on those who yield themselves to its beauty.

L E T T E R

42

A Cloud of Witnesses

Are you surprised to learn that there is even a greater difference between the beings in this world than between the people of earth? That is inevitable, for this is a freer world than yours.

I should fail in my duty if I did not tell you something of the unfriendly beings out here; perhaps no one else will ever tell you, and the knowledge is necessary to self-protection.

First I want to say that there is a strong sympathy between the spirits in this world and the spirits in your world. Yes, they are both spirits, the difference being mainly a difference in garments, one wearing flesh and the other wearing a subtler but nonetheless real body.

Now the congenial spirits, which may be the "spirits of just men made perfect," or those who merely aspire to perfection, are powerfully drawn to those fellow spirits on earth whose ideals are in harmony with their own. The magnetic attraction which exists between human beings is weak compared with that which is possible between beings embodied and beings disembodied. As opposites attract, the very difference in matter is a drawing force. The female is not more attractive to the male than the being of flesh is attractive to the being in the astral. The two do not usually understand each other; neither do man and woman. But the influence is felt, and beings out here understand its source better than you do, because they generally carry with them the memory of your world, while you have lost the memory of theirs.

At no time is the sympathetic power between men and spirits so strong as when men are laboring under some intense emotion, be it love or hate, or anger, or any other excitement. For then the fiery element in man is most active, and spirits are attracted by fire.

(*Here the writing suddenly stopped, the influence passed, to return after a few minutes.*)

You wonder why I went away? It was in order to draw a wide protective circle around us both, for what I have to say to you is something which certain spirits would wish me to leave unsaid.

To continue. When man is excited, exalted, or in any way intensified in his emotional life, the spirits draw near to him. That is how conception is possible; that is the secret of inspiration; that is why anger grows with what it feeds upon.

And this last is the point which I want to drive home to your consciousness. When you lose your temper, you lose a great deal, among other things *the control of yourself,* and it is barely possible that another entity may momentarily assume control of you.

This subjective world, as I have called it, has its share of inimical spirits. They love to stir up strife, both here and on earth. They enjoy the excitement of anger in others; they are thrilled by the poison of hatred. As certain men revel in morphine, so they revel in all inharmonious passion.

Do you see the point and the danger? A small seed of anger in your heart they feed and inflame by the hatred in their own. It is not necessarily hatred of you as an individual; often they have no personal interest in you; but for the purpose of gratifying their hostile passion they will attach themselves to you temporarily. Other illustrations are not far to seek.

A man who has the habit of anger, even of fault-finding, is certain to be surrounded by antagonistic spirits. I have seen a score of them around a man, thrilling him with their own malignant magnetism, stirring him up again when by reaction he would have cooled down.

Sometimes the impersonal interest in mere strife becomes personal; an angry spirit here may find that by attaching himself to a certain man he is sure to get every day a thrill or thrills of angry excitement, as his victim continually loses his temper and storms and rages. This is one of the most terrible misfortunes which can happen to anybody. Carried to its ultimate, it may become obsession, and end in insanity.

The same law applies to other unlovely passions, those of lust and avarice. Beware of lust, beware of all sex attraction into which no spiritual or heart element enters. I have seen things that I would not wish to record, either through your hand or any other.

Let us take instead a case of avarice. I have seen a miser counting over his gold, have seen the rapacious eyes of the spirits which enjoyed the gold through him. For gold has a peculiar influence as a metal, apart from its purchasing power or the associations attached to it. Certain spirits love gold, even as the miser loves it, and with the same acquisitive, astringent passion. As it is one of the heaviest of metals, so its power is a condensed and condensing power.

I do not mean by this that you should beware of gold. Get all you can use, for it is useful; but do not gloat over it. One does not attract the avaricious spirits merely by owning the symbols of wealth—houses and lands and stocks and bonds, or even a moderate amount of coin; but I advise you not to hoard coins to gloat over.

There are certain jewels, however, whose possession will aid you, for they attract the spirits of power. But you will probably choose your jewels by reason of your affinity with them, and may choose wisely.

Now that I have done my duty by warning you against the passions and the passionate spirits of which you should beware, I can go on to speak of other feelings and of other spiritual associates of man.

You have met persons who seemed to radiate sunshine, whose very presence in a room made you happier. Have you asked yourself why? The true answer would be that by their lovely disposition they attracted round them a "cloud of witnesses" as to the joy and the beauty of life.

I have myself often basked in the warm rays of a certain loving heart I know upon the earth. I have heard spirits say to one another as they crowded round that person, "It is good to be here." Do you think that any unsavory thing could happen to him? A score of loving and sympathetic spirits would strive to give him warning should any harm threaten.

Then, too, a joyous heart attracts joyous events.

Simplicity, also, and sweet humility, are very attractive to gentle disembodied souls. "Except ye be as little children, ye cannot enter in."

Have you not often seen a child enjoying himself with unseen playfellows? You would call them imaginary playfellows. Perhaps they were, perhaps they were not imaginary. To imagine may be to create, or it may be to attract things already created.

I have seen the Beautiful Being itself, more than once, hovering in ecstasy above an earthly creature who was happy.

A song of joy, when it comes from a thrilling heart, may attract a host of invisible beings who enjoy it with the singer; for, as I have told you, sound carries from one world to another.

Never weep—unless you must, to restore lost equilibrium. The weeping spirits, however, are rather harmless because they are weak. Sometimes a storm of tears, when it is past, clears the soul's atmosphere; but while the weeping is in progress, the atmosphere is thick with weeping spirits. One could almost hear the drip of their tears through the veil of ether—if

213

•

the sobbing earthly one did not make so much noise with his grief.

"Laugh and the world laughs with you," may be true enough; but when you weep, you do *not* weep alone.

L E T T E R
43

The Kingdom Within

There is one obscure point which I want to make clear, even though I may be accused of "mysticism" by those to whom mysticism means only obscurity.

I have said that the life of man is both subjective and objective, but principally objective; and that the life of "spirits" dwelling in subtle matter is both subjective and objective, but principally subjective.

Yet I have spoken of going alone or with others to heaven, as a place. I want to explain this. You remember the saying, "The kingdom of heaven is within you," that is, subjective. Also, "Where two or three are gathered together in My name, there will I be in the midst of them."

Now, those places in this subtle realm which I have called the Christian heavens are places where two or three, or two or three thousand, as the case may be, are gathered together in His name, to enjoy the *kingdom of heaven within them*.

The aggregation of souls is objective—that is, the souls exist in time and space; the heaven which they enjoy is subjective, though they may all see the same thing at the same time, as, for instance, the vision of Him whom they adore as Redeemer.

That is as clear as I can make it.

L E T T E R
44

The Game of Make-Believe

One day I met a man in doublet and hose, who announced to me that he was Shakespeare. Now I have become accustomed to such announcements, and they do not surprise me as they did six or eight months ago. (Yes, I still keep account of your months, for a purpose of my own.)

I asked this man what proof he could adduce of his extraordinary claim, and he answered that it needed no proof.

"That will not go down with me," I said, "for I am an old lawyer."

Thereupon he laughed, and asked:

"Why did you not join in the game?"

I am telling you this rather senseless story, because it illustrates an interesting point in regard to our life here.

In a former letter I wrote about my meeting with a newly arrived lady, who, finding me dressed in a Roman toga, thought that I might be

Caesar; and that I told her we were all actors here. I meant that, like children, we "dress up" when we want to impress our own imagination, or to relive some scene in the past.

This playing of a part is usually quite innocent, though sometimes the very ease with which it is done brings with it the temptation to deception, especially in dealings with the earth people.

You see the point I wish to make. The "deceitful spirits," of which the frequenters of séance rooms so often make complaint, are these astral actors, who may even come to take a certain pride in the cleverness of their art.

218

Be not too sure that the spirit who claims to be your deceased grandfather is that estimable old man himself. He may be merely an actor playing a part, for his own entertainment and yours.

How is one to tell, you ask? One cannot always tell. I should say, however, that the surest test of all would be the deep and *unemotional* conviction that the veritable entity was in one's presence. There is an instinct in the human heart which will never deceive us, if we without fear or bias will yield ourselves to its decision. How often in worldly matters have we all acted against this inner monitor, and been deceived and led astray!

•

If you have an instinctive feeling that a certain invisible—or even visible—entity is not what it claims to be, it is better to discontinue the conference. If it is the real person, and if he has anything vital to say, he will come again and again; for the so-called dead are often very desirous to communicate with the living.

As a rule, though, the play-acting over here is innocent of intent to deceive. Most men desire occasionally to be something which they are not. The poor man who, for one evening, dresses himself in his best clothes and squanders a week's salary in playing the millionaire is moved by the same impulse which inspired the man in my story to assert that he was Shakespeare. The woman who always dresses beyond her means is playing the same little game with herself and with the world.

All children know the game. They will tell you in a convinced tone that they are Napoleon Bonaparte, or George Washington, and they feel hurt if you scoff.

Perhaps my friend with the Shakespearean aspiration was an amateur dramatist when he was on earth. Had he been a professional dramatist, he would probably have stated his real name, more or less unknown, and followed it by the declaration that he was the well-known So-and-so.

•

THE GAME OF MAKE-BELIEVE

There is much pride out here in the accomplishments of the earth life, especially among those who have recently come out. This lessens with time, and after one has been long here, one's interests are likely to be more general.

Men and women do not cease to be human merely by crossing the frontier of what you call the invisible world. In fact, the human characteristics are often exaggerated, because the restraints are fewer. There are no penalties inflicted by the community for the personating of one man by another. It is not taken seriously, for to the clearer sight of this world the disguise is too transparent.

220

L E T T E R
45

HEIRS OF HERMES

There is much sound sense and not a little nonsense talked about Adepts and Masters, who live and work on the astral plane. Now I am myself living, and sometimes working, on the so-called astral plane, and what I say about the plane is the result of experience and not of theory.

I have met Adepts—yes, Masters here. One of them especially has taught me much, and has guided my footsteps from the first.

Do not fear to believe in Masters. Masters are men raised to the highest power; and whether they are embodied or disembodied, they work on this plane of life. A Master can go in and out at will.

No, I am not going to tell the world how they do it. Some who are not Masters might try the experiment, and not be able to go back again. Knowledge is power; but there are certain powers which may be dangerous if put in practice without a corresponding degree of wisdom.

•

All human beings have in them the potentiality of mastership. That ought to be an encouragement to men and women who aspire to an intensity of life beyond that of the ordinary. But the attainment of mastership is a steady and generally a slow growth.

My Teacher here is a Master.

There are teachers here who are not Masters, as there are teachers on earth who have not the rank of professor; but he who is willing to teach what he knows is on the right road.

I do not mind saying that my Teacher approves of my trying to tell the world something about the life which follows the change that is called death. If he disapproved, I should bow to his superior wisdom.

No, it does not matter what his name is. I have referred to him simply as my Teacher, and have told you many things which he has said and done. Many other things I have not told you, for I can only come occasionally now. After a time I shall probably cease to come altogether. Not that I shall have lost interest in you; but it seems to be the plan that I shall get farther away from the world, to learn things which necessitate for their comprehension a certain loosening of the earthly tie. Later I may return again, for the second time; but I make no promises. I will come if I can, and if it seems wise to come, and if you are in a mood to let me.

I do not believe that I shall come through anybody else—at least, not to write letters like this. I should probably have to put such another person through the same training process that I put you through, and few—even those who were my friends and associates—would trust me to that extent. So, even after I am gone, do not shut the door too tight, in case I should want to come again, for I might have something immensely important to say. But, on the other hand, please refrain from calling me; because if you should call me you might draw me away from important work or study somewhere else. I do not say for certain that you could, but it is possible; and when I leave the neighborhood of the earth of my own accord, I do not wish to be drawn back until I am ready to return.

A person still upon the earth may call so intensely to a friend who has passed far away from the earth's atmosphere, that that soul will come back too soon in response to the eager cry.

Do not forget the dead, unless they are strong enough to be happy without your remembrance; but do not lean too heavily upon them.

The Masters, of whom I spoke a little while ago, can remain near or far away, as they will; they can respond or not respond: but the ordinary soul is very sensitive to the call of those it loved on earth.

I have seen a mother respond eagerly to the tearful prayer of a child, and yet unable to make the lonely one realize her presence. Sometimes the mothers are very sad because they cannot make their presence felt.

One time I saw my Teacher by his power help a mother to make herself seen and heard by a daughter who was in great trouble. The heart of my Teacher is very soft to the sufferings of the world; and though he says that he is not one of the Christs, yet he often seems to work as Christ works. At other times he is all mind. He illustrates the saying about the thrice-greatest Hermes Trismegistus—great in body, great in mind, great in heart.

I wish I could tell you more about my Teacher, but he does not wish to be too well known on earth. He works for the work's sake, and not for reward or praise.

He is very fond of children, and one day when I was sitting unseen in the house of a friend of mine on earth, and the little son of the house fell down and hurt himself and wept bitterly, my great Teacher, whom I have seen command literally "legions of angels," bent down in his tenuous form, which he was then wearing, and soothed and comforted the child.

•

When I asked him about it afterwards, he said that he remembered many childhoods of his own, in other lands, and that he could still feel in memory the sting of physical pain and the shock of a physical fall.

He told me that children suffer more than their elders realize, that the bewilderment felt in gradually adjusting to a new and frail and growing body is often the cause of intense suffering.

He said that the constant crying of some small babies is caused by their half-discouragement at the herculean task before them—the task of molding a body through which their spirit can work.

He told me a story of one of his former incarnations, before he became a Master, and what a hard struggle he had to build a body. He could remember even the smallest details of that faraway life. One day his mother punished him for something which he had not really done, and when he denied the supposed wrongful act, she chided him for untruthfulness, not realizing—good woman though she was—the essential truth of the soul to whom she had given form. He told me that from that childish impression, centuries ago, he could date his real battle against injustice, which had helped to develop him as a friend and teacher of mankind.

Then he went on to speak of the importance of our recovering the memory of other lives, in

225

order that we may see the roads by which our souls have come.

As a rule, the great Teachers are reticent about their own past, and they only refer to it when some point in their experience can be used to illustrate a principle, and thus help another to grasp the principle. It encourages a groping soul to know that one who has attained a great height has been through the same trials that now perplex him.

L E T T E R
46

Only a Song

Will you listen to another song, or chant, or whatever you choose to call it, of that amazing angel whom we know as the Beautiful Being?

Why do you fear to question me? I am the great answerer of questions;

Though my answers are often symbols, yet words themselves are only symbols.

I have not visited you for a season, for when I am around, you can think of nothing else, and it is well that you should think of those who have trodden the path you are treading.

You can pattern your ways on those of others; you can hardly pattern your ways on mine.

I am a light in the darkness—my name you do not need to know;

A name is a limitation, and I refuse to be limited.

In the ancient days of the angels, I refused to enter the forms of my own creation, except to play with them.

There is a hint for you, if you like hints.

He who is held by his own creations becomes a slave. That is one of the differences between me and men.

What earthly father can escape his children? What earthly mother wishes to?

But I! I can make a rose to bloom—then leave it for another to enjoy.

My joy was in the making. It would be dull for me to stay with a rose until its petals fell.

228

The artist who can forget his past creations may create greater and greater things.

The joy is in the doing, not in the holding fast to that which is done.

Oh, the magic of letting go! It is the magic of the gods.

There are races of men to whom I have revealed myself. They worship me.

You need not worship me, for I do not require worship.

That would be to limit myself to my own creations, if I needed anything from the souls I have touched with my beauty.

Oh, the magic of letting go!

●

ONLY A SONG

The magic of holding on?

Yes, there is a magic in holding on to a thing until it is finished and perfect;

But when a thing is finished, whether it be a poem, a love, or a child, let it go.

In that way you are free again and may begin another. It is the secret of eternal youth.

Never look back with regret; look back only to learn what is behind you.

Look forward always; it is only when a man ceases to look forward to things that he begins to grow old. He settles down.

I have said to live in the moment; that is the same thing seen from another side.

The present and the future are playfellows; we do not play when we study the past.

I am the great playfellow of men.

LETTER

47

INVISIBLE GIFTS AT YULETIDE

It is not yet too late to wish you a merry Christmas.

How do I know that it is Christmas Day? Because I have been looking in at houses which I used to frequent, and have seen trees laden with tinsel and gifts. Do you wonder that I could see them? If so, you forget that we light our own place. When we know how to look, we can see behind the veil.

This is my first Christmas Day on this side. I cannot send you a material gift which you could wear or hang up in your room; but I can send you the good wishes of the season.

The mothers who have left young children behind them in the world know well when Christmas is approaching. Sometimes they bring invisible gifts, which they have fashioned by their power of imagination and love out of the tenuous matter of this world. A certain grandmother all last evening, Christmas Eve, was

•

scattering flowers around her dear ones. Their fragrance must have penetrated the atmosphere of the earth.

Did you ever smell suddenly a sweet perfume which you could not account for? If so, perhaps some one who loved you was scattering invisible flowers. Love is stronger than death.

Another whom you know will go out before long. Strengthen her with your faith.

The practice of keeping Christmas is a good one, if you do not forget the real meaning of the day. To some it means the birth into the world of the spirit of humility and love; but while love and humility had visited the world before the appearance of Jesus of Nazareth, yet never before nor since have they come with greater power than they came to Judea. Whether the stable in Bethlehem was a physical reality or a symbol, makes no difference.

I have been to the heavens of Christ, and know their beauty. "In my Father's house are many mansions."

A traveler like me who wishes to go to some particular heaven must first feel in himself what those souls feel who enjoy that heaven; then he can enter and commune with them. He could never go as a mere sightseer. That is why, as a rule, I have avoided the hells; but the heavens I often visit.

●

And I have been in purgatory, the purgatory of the Roman Catholics. Do not scoff at those who have masses said for the repose of the souls of the departed. The souls are often conscious of such thoughtfulness. They hear the music, and they *may* smell the incense; most of all, they feel the power of the thought directed to them. Purgatory is real, in the sense of being a real experience. If you want to call it a dream, you may; but dreams are sometimes terribly real.

Even those who do not believe in purgatory sometimes wander awhile in sadness, until they have adjusted themselves to the new conditions under which they live. Should one tell them that they were in purgatory, they might deny the existence of such a state; but they would readily admit their discomfort.

The surest way to escape that painful period of transition is to go into the hereafter with a full faith in immortality, a full faith in the power of the soul to create its own conditions.

Last night, after visiting various places upon the earth, I went to one of the highest Christian heavens. Perhaps I could not have gone so easily at any other time; for my heart was full of love for all men, and my mind was full of the Christ *idea*.

Often have I seen Him who is called the Savior of men, and last night I saw Him in all His beauty. He, too, came down to the world for a time.

I wonder if I can make you understand? The
love of Christ is always present in the world,
because there are always hearts that keep it
alight. If the idea of Christ as a redeemer should
ever grow faint in the world, He would probably
go back there and relight the flame in human
hearts; but whatever the writers of statistics may
say, that idea was never more real than at present. It may have been more talked about.

The world is not in so bad a way as some
people think. Be not surprised if there should be
a strong renaissance of the spiritual idea. All
things have their rhythms.

Last night I stood in a great church where
hundreds of Christians knelt in adoration of
Jesus. I have stood in churches on Christmas Eve
when on earth as a man among men; but I saw
things last night which I had never seen before.
Surely where two or three are gathered together
in the name of any prophet, there he is in the
midst of them, if not always in his spiritual body,
at least in the fragrance of his sympathy.

The angels in the Christian heavens know
when Christmas is being celebrated on earth.

Jesus of Nazareth is a reality. As a spiritual
body, as Jesus who dwelt in Galilee, He exists
in space and time; as the Christ, the paradigm
of the spiritual man, He exists in the hearts of
all men and women who awaken that idea in

themselves. He is a light which is reflected in many pools.

I wrote the other day about Adepts and Masters. Jesus is a type of the greatest Master. He is revered in all the heavens. He grasped the Law and dared to live it, to exemplify it. And when He said, "The Father and I are one," He pointed the way by which other men may realize mastership in themselves.

Humanity on its long road has evolved many Masters. Who then shall dare to question that humanity has justified itself? If one demands to know what purpose there is in life, tell him that it is this very evolution of the Master out of the man. Eternity is long. The goal is ahead for each unit of sufficient strength, and those who cannot lead can serve.

This thought came home to me with special force last night. I am not so bold as to say that every unit in the great mass is strong enough, has energy enough, to evolve individual mastership; but there is no unit so weak that it may not have some part, however small, in the great work of evolving Masters out of men. It is sweet to serve. They too have their reward.

The great mistake made by most minds in wrestling with the problem of evolution is in not grasping the fact that eternity is eternity, that to be immortal is to have no beginning or end.

There is time enough in which to develop, if not in this life cycle, then in another which will follow; for rhythm is sure.

If I could only make you grasp the idea of immortality as I see it! I did not fully understand it until I came out here and began to pick up the threads of my own past. My reason told me that I was immortal, but I did not know what immortality meant. I wonder if you do?

I know an angel who has done more, perhaps, than many prophets have done to keep that idea alight in the world. Until I met the one whom we know as the Beautiful Being, I had not reveled in the triumph of immortality. There is one who plays with immortality as a child plays with marbles.

When the Beautiful Being says, "I am," you know that you are, too. When the Beautiful Being says, "I pluck the centuries as a child pulls the petals of a daisy, and I throw away the seed-bearing heart to grow more century-bearing daisies," you feel—but words are weak to express what the Beautiful Being's joy in endless life can make one feel.

You forget the thing of flesh and bones which you used to call yourself when this sliver of conscious immortality exults in its own existence.

When the Beautiful Being takes you for a walk in what it calls the "clover meadows of the sky," you are quite sure that you are one of the co-heirs of the whole eternal estate.

The Beautiful Being knows well the Christ of the Christians. I think the Beautiful Being knows all the great Masters, embodied or disembodied. They all taught immortality in some form or other, if only in essence.

The Beautiful Being went with me last night to the highest heaven of the Christians. Should I tell you all that I saw, you might be in too great a hurry to go out there and view it for yourself, and you must not leave the earth for a long time yet. You must realize immortality while still in the flesh, and make others realize it.

236

I have told you about the minor heavens, where merely good people go; but the passionately devout lovers of God reach heights of contemplation and ecstasy which the words of the world's languages were not designed to describe. With the Beautiful Being at my side, I felt those ecstasies last night, while you were locked in sleep.

Where shall I be next Christmas Eve? I shall be somewhere in the universe; for we could not get out of the universe if we should try. The universe could not get on without us; it would be incomplete. Take that thought with you into the happy New Year.

L E T T E R
48

THE GREATER DREAMLAND

I have not been to see you for some time, for
I have been trying an experiment.

Since coming to this country, I have so often
seen men and women lying in a state of subjective enjoyment, of dream, if I may use the word,
that I have long wanted to spend a few days
alone with my interior self, in that same state. My
reason for hesitating was that I feared to dream
too long, and thus to lose valuable time—both
yours and mine.

But when I expressed to the Teacher one
day my desire to visit the greater dreamland
lying within my own brain, also my fear that I
might be slow in waking, he promised that he
would come and wake me in exactly seven
days of earthly time if I had not already
aroused myself.

"For," he said, "you can set an alarm clock
in your own brain, which can always be relied
upon."

This I knew from old experience; but I had feared that the psychic sleep might be deeper than the ordinary earthly sleep, and that the alarm clock might not go off at the appointed time.

I have heard much comment, so doubtless have you, on the fact that spirits, when they return to communicate with their friends, say, as a rule, so little about their celestial life. The reason is, I fancy, that they despair of making themselves understood should they attempt to describe their existence, which is so different from that of earth.

Now, most souls, when they have been out some time, fall into that state of reverie, or dream, which I had so long desired to experience for myself. Some souls awake at intervals, and show an occasional interest in the things and people of the earth; but if the sleep is deep, and if the soul is willing or desirous to leave the things of the earth behind, the subconscious state may last uninterruptedly for years, or even centuries. But a soul that could stay asleep for centuries would probably be one that was living according to long rhythm, the normal rhythm of humanity.

So, when I went into the deep sleep, I went into it with a spell upon myself not to remain too long.

Oh, it was wonderful, that dream-country in my own self! The Theosophists would perhaps say that I had taken a rest in the bliss of devachan. No matter what one calls it. It was an experience worth remembering.

I closed my eyes and went in—in—deeper than thought, where the restless waves of life are still, and the soul is face to face with itself and with all the wonders of its own past. There is nothing but loveliness in that sleep. If one can bring back the dreams, as I did, the sojourn there is an adventure beyond comparison.

I went in to enjoy, and I enjoyed. I found there the simulacrum of everyone whom I had ever loved. They smiled at me, and I understood the mystery of them, and why we had been drawn together.

239

I refound, too, my old dreams of ambition, and enjoyed the fruit of all my labor on earth. It is a rosy world, that inner world of the soul, and the heart's desire is always found there. No wonder that the strenuous life of earth is oftener than not a pain and a travail, for the dream-life which follows is so beautiful that the balance must be preserved.

Rest! On earth you know not the meaning of the word. I rested only seven days; but so refreshed was I that, had I not other worlds to conquer, I should almost have had the courage to return to earth.

•

Do not neglect rest—you who still live the toilsome life in the sunshine. For every added hour of true rest your working capacity is increased. Have no fear. You are not wasting time when you lie down and dream. As I have said before, eternity is long. There is room for rest in the wayside inns which dot the path which the cycles tread.

If you want to take a long and devachanic rest—why, take it. Take it even on earth, if it seems desirable. Do not be always grubbing, even at literature. Go out and play with the squirrels, or lie by the fire and dream with the household cat. The cat that enjoys the drowsy fireside also enjoys catching mice when the mood is on her. She cannot be always hunting; neither can you.

Just take a dip in devachan some day, and see how refreshed you will be when you come out. Perhaps I am misusing that word "devachan," for I was never very deeply learned in the lore of Theosophy.

I have even heard nirvana described as a state of intense motion, so rapid that it seems motionless, like a spinning top, or the wing of a hummingbird. But nirvana is not for all men— not yet.

I have hinted at the wonders of my seven days of blissful rest, but I have not described them. How can I? A great poet once declared that there was no thought or feeling which could not be expressed in words. Perhaps he has changed his mind by this time, after being out here some sixty years.

As I went to rest, I commanded my soul to bring back every dream. Of course I cannot say whether some may not have escaped, any more than you can say on waking that you have or have not forgotten the deeper experiences of the night. But when I came back into the normal life of this plane that is called astral, I felt like an explorer who returns from a strange journey with wonder-tales to tell. Only I did not tell them. To whom should I relate those dreams and visions? I would not be a bore, even to "disembodied" associates. Had Lionel been here, I might have entertained him many an hour with my stories; but he is lost to me for the present.

And, by the way, he seems to have taken little or no devachanic rest. Is that because he was so young on coming out that he had not exhausted the normal rhythm? Probably. Had he remained out here and grown up, perhaps he also would have sought the deeper interior world. But I will not speculate, for this is a record of experiences, not of speculations. You can speculate as well as I, if you think it worthwhile.

I found in my own dreamland a fair, fair face. No, I am not going to tell you about that; it is my little secret. Of course I found many faces, but one was lovelier than all the others, and it was not the face of the Beautiful Being, either. The Beautiful Being I meet when I am wide awake. I did not encounter her as an actual presence in sleep, only the simulacrum of her. In the deeper dreamland we see only what is in our brains. *Things* do not exist there, only the memories of things and the imagination of them.

Imagination creates in this world, as in yours: it actually molds the tenuous substance; but in the greater dreamland I do not think that we mold in substance. It is a world of light and shadow pictures, too subtle to be described.

Even before this experience, I had gone into the memories of my own past; but I had not reveled in them, had not indulged myself to the extent of conjuring with light and shade. But, oh! what's the use? There are no words to describe it. Can you describe the perfume of a rose, as you once said yourself? Can you tell how a kiss feels? Could you even describe the emotion of fear so that one who had not felt it, by former experience in this life or some other, would know what you meant? No more can I describe the process of spiritual dreaming.

Revel to your heart's content in fancy, in memory, while you are still in the body, and yet I think that you will have only the shadow of a shadow of what I experienced in those seven days, the reflection of a reflection of the real dream. The reflection of a reflection! I like that phrase. It suggests a clear picture, though not a direct impression. Try dreaming, then, even on earth, and maybe you will get a reflection of a reflection of the pictured joys of the spiritual dreamland.

243

L E T T E R
49

A Sermon and a Promise

As I have been coming to you every few days for several months, and have told stories for your amusement, may I come now and preach a sermon? I promise it shall not be long.

You live in a land where church spires pierce the blue of heaven, looking from the viewpoint of the clouds like the uplifted spears of an invading army—which in intent they are; so surely you have the habit of listening to sermons. The average sermon is made up mostly of advice, and mine will not differ from others in that particular. I wish to advise you, and as many other persons as you can make listen to my advice.

You will grant that, for one who offers counsel, I have had unusual opportunities for fitting myself to give it. In order to help you to live, I would show you the point of view of a serious and thoughtful—however imperfect—observer of the aftereffects of causes set in motion by dwellers upon the earth. It has been said that cause and effect are opposite and equal. Very good. Now I want to draw your attention to certain illustrations of that axiom which have come to my mind during the last few months. If I repeat one or two things which I have already said, that is no serious matter. You may have forgotten them, or missed their application to the business of preparing for the future life on this side of the gulf of death. That is a moss-grown figure of speech, "the gulf of death"; but I am writing a sermon, not a poem, and well-worn tropes are expected from the pulpit.

The preachers remind you every few Sundays that you have got to die some day. Do you realize it? Does your consciousness take in the fact that at any moment—tomorrow or fifty years hence—you may suddenly find yourself *outside* that body whose cohesive force you have become accustomed to; that you may find yourself, either alone or accompanied, in a very tenuous and light and at first not easily manageable body, with no certain power of communicating with those friends and relations whom you may see in the very room with you?

You have not realized it! Then get it through your consciousness. Grasp it with both hemispheres of your brain. Clutch it with the talons of your mind. *You are going to die.*

Oh, do not be alarmed! I do not mean you personally, nor that you, or any particular person, will die tomorrow or next year; but die you must some day; and if you remind yourself of it occasionally, it will lessen the shock of the actual happening when it comes.

Do not brood over the thought of death. God forbid that you should read such a morbid meaning into my blunt words! But be prepared. You insure your life for so much money that your family may be provided for; but you do nothing to insure your own future peace of mind regarding your own self.

Remember this always: however minute are the instructions you leave for the management of your affairs after death, should you be able to look back to the earth, you will find that someone has mismanaged them. So expect just that, take it as a matter of course, and learn to say, "What difference does it make?" Learn to feel that the past *is* past, that the future alone has possibilities for you, and that the sooner you leave other persons to manage your discarded earthly affairs, the better it will be for your own tranquility. Be prepared to *let go*. That is the first point I wish to make.

Do not go out into the new life with only one eye open to the celestial planes, and the other inverted towards the images of earth. You will not get far if you do. Let go. Get away from the world just as soon as you can.

246

This may sound to some people like heartless advice, for there is no doubt that a wise spirit, looking down from the higher sphere, can, by his subtly instilled telepathic suggestions, influence for good the men and women of the earth. But there are always thousands of those who are eager to do that. The heavens above your head now are literally swarming with souls who long to take a hand in the business of earth, souls who cannot let go, who find the habit of managing other people's affairs a fascinating habit, as enthralling as that of tobacco, or opium. Again, do not call me heartless. I am blunt of speech, but I love you, men of earth. If I hurt you, it is for your good.

Now comes another and a most interesting point. Forget, if you can, the sins you have committed in the flesh. You cannot escape the effects of those causes; but you can avoid strengthening the tie with sin, you can avoid going back to earth self-hypnotized with the idea that you are a sinner.

Do not brood over sin. It is true that you can exhaust the impulse to sin by dwelling on it until your soul is disgusted; but that is a slow and an unpleasant process. The shortcut of forgetfulness is better.

Now I want to express an idea very difficult to express, for the reason that it will be quite new to most of you. It is this: The power of the creative imagination is stronger in men wearing their earthly bodies than it is in men (spirits) who have laid off their bodies. Not that most persons know how to use that power; they do not. The point I wish to make is that they *can* use it. A solid body is a resistive base, a powerful lever, from which the will can project those things conjured by the imagination. That is, I believe, the real reason why Masters retain their physical bodies. The trained mind, robed in the tenuous matter of our world, is stronger than the untrained mind robed in dense matter; but the Master still robed in flesh can command a legion of angels.

248

This is by way of preface to the assertion that as you on earth picture your future life to be, so it will be, limited always by the power with which you back your will, and by the possibility of subtle matter to take the mold you give it, and that possibility is almost unlimited.

Will to progress after death, and you will progress; will to learn, and you will learn; will to return to earth after a time to take up a special work, and you will return and take up that work.

Karma is an iron law, yes; but you are the creator of karma.

Above all things, do not expect—which is to demand—unconsciousness and annihilation. You cannot annihilate the unit of force which you are, but you can by self-suggestion put it to sleep for ages. Go out of life with the determination to retain consciousness, and you will retain it.

When the time comes for you to enter that rest which a certain school of thought has called devachan, you will enter it; but that time will not be immediately after you go out.

On finally reaching that state you will, as a matter of course, relive in dream your former earthly life and assimilate its experiences; but by that time you will have got rid of the desire personally to take part, as a spirit, in the lives of those you have left behind.

Do not, while still on earth, invoke the spirits of the dead. They may be busy elsewhere, and you may be strong enough to call them away from their own business to attend to yours unwillingly.

You who write for me, I want to thank you for never calling me. You let me come always at my own time, and let me say what I wish to say without confusing my thought by either questions or comments.

You of the earth who are still upon the earth may find your departed friends when you come out here, if they have not already put on another body. Meantime, let them perform the work of the state in which they are.

•

You who write for me will remember that the first time I came you did not even know that I had left the earth. I found you in a passive mood, and wrote a message signed by a symbol whose special meaning was unknown to you, but which I knew would be immediately recognized by those in whom you were likely to confide. That was a most fortunate beginning, for it gave you confidence in the genuineness of my communications.

But I said that I would write only a sermon tonight, so I will now pronounce the blessing and depart. I shall return, however. This is not the last meeting of the season.

Later.

One word more before I go to my other work.

If you had urgently called me during that week which I spent in rest, you might have had the power to cut short a most interesting and valuable experience. So the final word, after the benediction of this sermon, is: Do not be too egotistically insistent, even with the so-called dead.

If your need is great, the souls who love you may feel it and come to you of their own accord. This is often illustrated in the earth life, among those whose psychic pores are open.

•

L E T T E R
5O

THE APRIL OF THE WORLD

Having told you last week that you must die, according to the jargon of the earth, I now want to assure you that you can never really die at all; that you are as immortal as the angels, as immortal as God Himself.

No, that is not a contradiction.

I have spoken before of immortality; it was always a favorite theme of mine; but since my association with the Beautiful Being, it has become for me an exultant consciousness.

The Beautiful Being lives in eternity, as we fancy that we live in time. Will you write down here another of that angel's chants?

When you see me in the green trees and in the green
    light under trees, know that you are near to me;

When you hear my voice in the silence, know that I
    speak for you.

•

The immortal loves to speak to the immortal in the mortal, and there is joy in calling to the joy which dozes in the heart of a soul of earth.

When joy is awake, the soul is awake.

You look for God in the forms of men and women, and sometimes you find Him there;

But you look for me in your own soul; the deeper the gaze, the fairer the vision.

Yes, I am in Nature, and I am in you, when you look for me there;

For Nature is dual, and the half you carry within you.

All things are one and dual—even I, and that is why you may find me.

Oh, the charm of being free, to wander at will round the earth and heaven, and through the souls of men!

I am lighter than the thistle-down, but more enduring than the stars:

The permanent is impalpable, and only the impalpable endures.

The road is not long which leads to the castle of dreams; the far away is nearer than next door, but only the dreamer finds it.

When labor is light, the pay is sure; when the days are hard, their reward is tardy.

•

Be glad, and I will repay you.

I would write my name on the leaves of your heart, but only the angels can read the writing.

Who bears my unknown name on the petals of his heart is accepted among the angels for the flower he is; his perfume reaches heaven.

There is pollen in the heart, child of earth, and it fructifies the flowers of faith;

There is faith in the soul, child of time, and it bears the seeds of all things.

The seasons come and the seasons go, but the springtime is eternal.

I can find that in you which was lost in the April of the world.

•

L E T T E R

5I

A HAPPY WIDOWER

I met a charming woman the other night, quite different from anyone else I have met heretofore. She was no less a woman because she weighed perhaps a milligram instead of one hundred and thirty pounds.

I was passing along a quiet road, and saw her standing by a fountain. Who had created the fountain? I cannot say. There are sculptors in this world who mold for the love of the work more beautiful fountains than your sculptors mold for money. The joy of the workman in his work! Why, that *is* heaven, is it not?

I saw a beautiful woman standing by a fountain; and as I love beauty, whether in fountains or in women, I paused to regard both.

The lovelier of the two looked up and laughed.

"I was wishing for someone to talk to," she said. "What a wonderful world this is!"

"I am glad you find it so," I answered. "I also

do not agree with the old woman who declared that heaven was a much overrated place."

"You don't remember me, do you?" she asked.

"No. Have we met before?"

"We have. And, of course, you could remember me, if you should try."

Then I recalled who she was. We had met some years before on one of my journeys to New York, and I had talked with her about the mysteries of life and death, of will and destiny.

"I have tested many of the things you told me," she went on, "and I have found them true."

"What things, for instance?"

"First and most important, that man may create his own environment."

"You can easily demonstrate that here," I said. "But how long have you been in this world?"

"Only a few months."

"And how did you come out?"

"I died of too much joy."

"That was a pleasant death and an unusual one," I said, smiling. "How did it happen?"

"The doctor said that I died of heart failure. For years I had wanted a certain thing, and when it came to me suddenly, the realization was too much for me."

"And then?"

"Why, I suddenly realized that I had let slip the body through which I might have enjoyed this thing I had attained."

"And then?"

"I remembered that I was not my body, that I was my consciousness; and as long as that was intact, I was intact. So I went right on enjoying the attainment."

"Without a regret?"

"Yes."

"You are indeed a philosopher," I said. "And though I do not want to force your confidence, yet I would be much interested to know your story."

"It would seem absurd to some people," she answered, "and even to me it seems strange sometimes. But I had always wanted money, a great deal of money. One day a certain person died, leaving me a fortune. It was that joy which was too strong for me."

"And how do you enjoy the fortune here?"

"In several ways. My husband and I had planned a beautiful house—if we should ever have the money. We had planned to travel, too, and to see the interesting places of the world. We also had two or three friends who loved to create beauty in the arts, and who were hampered in their work by lack of means. Now, my husband, being my sole heir, came into the fortune immediately I passed out. So I enjoy everything with him and through him just the same as if I were actually in the flesh."

"And he knows that you are present?"

"Yes. We had each promised not to desert the other in life or death. I have kept my word, and he knows that I have kept it."

"And where is he now?"

"Traveling."

"Alone?"

"Except for me."

"In what place is he?"

"In Egypt at this time."

I drew nearer.

"Can you show him to me?" I asked.

"Yes, I think so. Come along."

It is needless to say that I did not require a second invitation.

We found the man—a handsome fellow about thirty years of age—sitting alone in a luxurious bedroom in Cairo. It seems to be my destiny to have strange experiences in Cairo!

The young man was reading as we entered the room; but he looked up at once, for he felt that *she* was there. I do not think he perceived me.

"My darling," he said, aloud, "I have seen the Pyramids!"

She placed her hand upon his forehead, and he closed his eyes, the better to see her.

Then his hand moved to the table, he opened his eyes again, and took up paper and pencil. I saw her guide his hand, which wrote:

"I have brought a friend with me. Can you see him?"

"No."

The man spoke aloud, she communicating through the pencil in his hand and by his interior perception of her.

"Then never mind," she wrote; "he is not an egotist. I only wanted him to see you. I have told him how happy I am—and now he sees why."

"This journey of mine is an unalloyed delight," the man said.

"That is because I am with you," she replied.

"Were you with me at the Pyramids today?"

"Yes, though I cannot see very well in the sunshine. I have been there, however, and have seen them by moonlight. But where are you going from here?"

"Where do you want me to go?"

"Up the Nile, to Aswan."

"I will go. When shall I start?"

"The day after tomorrow. And now *au revoir*, my love. I will return, by and by."

A moment later we were outside—she and I—in the soft starlight of an Egyptian evening.

"Did I not tell you the truth?" she demanded, with a little laugh of triumph.

●

"But have you no desire to go on in the spiritual world?" I asked.

"Is there anything more spiritual than love?" she asked in return. "Is not love the fulfilling of the Law?"

"But," I said, "I recently wrote a letter to the men and women of the earth, advising those who should come out here to get away from the earth as soon as possible."

"Lovers like me will not take your advice," she answered, with a smile. "And tell me now: Is it not better for Henry to enjoy my society in the long evenings—is it not better for him to be happy than to grieve for me?"

"But at first? Was he not inconsolable at your going out?"

"Yes, until I came to him. He was sitting one night in deep dejection, and I reached for his hand, and wrote with it: 'I am here. Speak to me.' 'My Love!' he cried, his face alight, 'are you really there?' 'Yes, I am here, and I shall come to you every day until you come out to me,' I answered, through the pencil.

"He had never known that he was what you call a 'writing medium.' He would never have been but for my presence in a form of matter different from his own.

"Come now, my friend," she added, "would you really advise me not to visit Henry any more?"

•

"There are said to be exceptions to all rules," I answered. "At this moment you seem to me to be one of those exceptions."

"And will you add a postscript to your recent letter to the world?"

"If I can," I said, "I will tell your story. My readers can draw their own conclusions."

"Thank you," was her answer.

"But," I added, "when Henry comes out here in his turn, you two together should go away from the world."

"Have *you* been away from the world then?"

"To some extent. I am only stopping here now until a certain work is finished."

"And then where are you going?"

"To visit other planets."

"Henry and I will do that, too, when he comes out."

Now, my friend, I tell you this story for whatever it is worth. There are cases like hers, where an earthly tie is all-compelling. But in the case of most persons, I stand by my original assertion and my original advice.

L E T T E R
52

The Archives of the Soul

I have spoken of a determination to visit other planets when my work of writing these letters is ended; but I must not neglect to say that I consider such journeys to and fro in the universe of far less spiritual value than those of other journeys which I have made and shall make into the deep places of my own self. Traveling in actual space and time is important to a man, that he may gain knowledge of other lands and peoples, see the differences between these peoples and himself, and learn the causes thereof; yet quiet meditation is even a greater factor in growth. If a man whose spiritual perceptions are open can do but one of these two things, it would be better for him to sit in a cabin in the backwoods and seek in his own soul for the secrets which it guards, than to travel without such self-examination to the ends of the earth.

•

Get acquainted with your own soul. Know why you do this or that, why you feel this or that. Sit quietly when in doubt about any matter, and let the truth rise from the deeps of yourself. Examine your motives always. Do not say, "I ought to do this act for such and such a reason; therefore I do it for that reason." Such argument is self-deception. If you do a kind act, ask yourself why. Perhaps you can find even in a kind action a hidden motive of self-seeking. If you should find such a motive, do not deny it to yourself. Acknowledge it to yourself, though you need not advertise it on the walls of your dwelling. Such a secret understanding will give you a greater sympathy and comprehension in judging the motives of others.

262

Strive always for the ideal; but do not label every emotion as an ideal emotion if it is not really that. Speak the truth to yourself. Until you can dare to do that, you will make little progress in the quest for your own soul.

Between earth lives is a good time to meditate, but one should form the habit of meditation while still in the flesh. Habits formed in the flesh have a tendency to continue after the flesh is laid aside. That is a reason why one should keep as free as possible from physical habits.

If my charming acquaintance who comes every night to her husband to write love messages through his hand would spend the greater part of her time in acquiring knowledge of this new world, so that she could enlighten him, then might their communion be an unmixed good; but I fear it is not so. Therefore I shall look for her again, and give her some fatherly advice. She has a quick and receptive mind, and I think she will listen to me. He would be interested in her experiences, if for no other reason than because they are hers. Yes, I shall have to find her again.

I have made wonderful discoveries in the archives of my own soul. There I have found the memories of all my past, back to a time almost unbelievably distant. In seeing how the causes set up in one life have produced their effects in another life, I have learned more than I shall learn on my coming tour of the planets.

Everything exists in the soul; all knowledge is there. Grasp that idea if you can. The infallible part of us is the hidden part, and it is for us to bring it to light. Do you understand now why I advise the disembodied to break away from the distractions and the dazzling mirages of the earthly life? Only in the stillness of detachment can the soul yield up her secrets. It is not that I am indifferent to earthly loves; on the contrary, I love more deeply than ever all those whom I loved on earth; but I realize that if I can love them wisely instead of unwisely, it will be better both for them and for me.

Yet the call of the earth is loud sometimes, and my heart answers from this side of the veil.

L E T T E R
53

A FORMULA FOR MASTERSHIP

My friend, I am going to leave you for a while—perhaps for a long time.

It seems to me that my immediate work with the earth is done. I want still further to lighten my load, to soar out upon the waves of ether—far—far—and to forget, in the thrill of exploration, that I shall some day have to make my way back to the world through the narrow straits of birth.

I am going out with the Beautiful Being on a voyage of discovery. My companion has taken this journey before, and can show me the way to many wonders.

There is a sadness in bidding you good-bye. Do you remember the last time you saw me in my old body? We neither of us thought that afternoon that we should next meet in a foreign country, and under conditions so strange that half the world will doubt that we have ever met again at all, and the other half will wonder if indeed we have really met.

Tell me, was I ever more real to you than I am this evening? While sitting with me in the days of the past, did you ever know less of what I should say a moment afterwards than you know now? Rack your brain as you will, you cannot tell what I am going to talk about. That will prove to *you*, at least, that I am as real as ever.

I want to leave a few messages. Tell . . . . And tell . . . . And some day tell my boy to live a brave and clean life. He will be watched over. Tell him that if sometimes he feels the interior guidance, not to be afraid to trust it. Tell him to look within for light.

For the present, I have not much more to say to the world at large. But I want you to publish these letters, leaving out only the very personal paragraphs.

Yes, I may not see you again for a long time. Do not be sad. When I am gone, perhaps another will come.

Do not close the door too tight; but guard well the door, and let no one enter who has not the signs and passwords. You will not be deceived; I have trained you to that end.

I cannot write much tonight, for there is sadness in leaving the earth. But I am—or shall be—all a-thrill with the interest of the coming voyage. Think of it! I shall see faraway planets and meet their inhabitants. Shall I find the "square-faced men"? Perhaps so.

In Jupiter, they say, there is a race of beings wonderful to behold. I shall see them. Will they be fairer than our own Beautiful Being, who loves the little earth and usually stays near it, because there are such struggles there?

The joy of the struggle! That is the keynote of immortality, the keynote of power. Let this be my final message to the world. Tell them to enjoy their struggles, to thrill at the endless possibilities of combination and creation, to live in the moment while preparing for long hence, and not to exaggerate the importance of momentary failures and disappointments.

267

When they come out here and get their lives in perspective, they will see that most of their causes of anxiety were trivial, and that all the lights and shadows were necessary to the picture.

I had my lights and shadows, too, but I regret nothing. The Master enjoys difficulties as a swimmer enjoys the resistance of the water.

If I could make you realize the power that comes from facing the struggle—not only bravely, as all the platitudinous bores will tell you, but facing it with enjoyment. Why, any healthy athlete enjoys a challenge.

Remember that your opponents are not other men, but conditions. If you fight men, they will

•

fight you back; but if you fight conditions, they, being unintelligent, will yield to you with just enough resistance to keep your muscles in good order.

There is nothing in this universe stronger than the will of man when it is directed by a powerful unit of force. Whatever your strength, make the most of it in the challenge of life.

And do not forget the law of rhythm—that is at the back of everything. Count on rhythm; it never has failed yet, and it never will. Watch for the high tides of yourself and flow up with them; when the inevitable low tides come, either rest or meditate. You cannot escape rhythm. You transcend it by working with it.

You can even turn and grow young, for time also has its tides; and there are many ripples in the long sea-swell of life.

I feel that I am leaving much unsaid. But I shall meet you again some day.

THE END

A F T E R W O R D

"X" conveyed his parting message to Elsa Barker in early 1913. For almost two years, she received no further communication from her astral correspondent. Then, in February of 1915, Ms. Barker was "suddenly made aware that 'X' stood in the room, and wished to write." Thus began the second volume of *Letters*, focusing on World War I, as seen from "the self-lighted world."

In the second volume, published in 1915, Elsa Barker wrote in her introduction:

> In that first book of "X," I did not state who the writer was, not feeling at liberty to do so without the consent of his family; but in the summer of 1914, while I was still living in Europe, a long interview with Mr. Bruce Hatch appeared in the *New York Sunday World,* in which he expressed the conviction that the "Letters" were genuine communications from his father, the late Judge David P. Hatch, of Los Angeles, California.

•

Who was Judge
Hatch? By all accounts,
he was "not an ordinary
man," as Ms. Barker her-
self described him. She
wrote: "He came nearer
than any other Occiden-
tal of my acquaintance
to that mastery of self
and of life which has
been called Adeptship."

Judge David Patterson Hatch

David Patterson Hatch was born in Dresden,
Maine, on November 22, 1846. When he was
eighteen, and following several years of illness,
his family decided to send him into the forests of
western Maine to learn camping, hunting, and
fishing as a way to regain his physical strength.
During this period, he not only recovered his
health, but developed an intense love of nature
that would stay with him his life long.

At the urging of his mother, he gave up his
decision to make hunting his profession and
entered Wesleyan Seminary, from which he graduated in 1871. After studying briefly at Michigan
Law School in Ann Arbor, he was admitted to law
practice in St. Paul, Minnesota, in 1872, and was
soon after appointed city attorney there. Three
years later, he moved to Santa Barbara, where in
1881 he was elected judge of the superior court.

•

AFTERWORD

A longtime associate and eventual successor to his law practice wrote a lengthy eulogy to Judge Hatch, whom he called "a philosopher of the soul." The following excerpts are taken from that published writing:

> Judge Hatch was a lawyer who did not practice law with his nose pressed down between the covers of his book. Rather his eyes looked out over its pages squarely into the face of Justice. . . . His knowledge of the principles of law was remarkable. . . .
>
> For about seven years he served as a judge of the superior court of Santa Barbara County. He resigned his judgeship to practice law in Los Angeles. His clientele was very diverse, ranging from some of the heaviest interests in Southern California down to the "charity work," much of which falls to the lot of every good lawyer. . . .
>
> Generally he was at his office early in the morning—at or before eight o'clock. But he burdened his mind very little with routine or rule. His favorite maxim was: "Whatever is, is right." At first, in my unfamiliarity with the depths of his philosophy, I got the idea that he used this expression as the slogan of fatalism. But later I came to understand him as meaning only that everything results according to natural law; that man of his own free will does the act, and that God, or Nature, has foreordained the law that is always cor-

rectly applied to every act; so that always a correct result ensues. . . .

Judge Hatch did not present to the world on Sunday any aspect of character or of conduct that he did not show to the world on Monday or Friday. His conduct of every day approached so closely the limits of his philosophy that, in my humble opinion, he taught it better by the acts of his daily life than by any word of mouth. He was less a hypocrite than any man with whom ever I had intimate association. He made no pretensions, and therefore had none to justify. More nearly he lived his philosophy than any preacher his creed. I say "philosophy," for to him creed and religion were but the lower steps of the pyramid, while the philosopher viewed the universe, and face to face talked to God. . . .

He was as gentle in speech as he was kind in heart, but he could say "No" shortly and gently, and mean it forever. Together for nearly ten years, the writer never received an unkind word from him; and, quite necessarily, had none to return. He seemed to be a man without stubbornness. If shown to be in error, he was as glad of the disclosure as he was prompt to rectify.

It is the writer's impression that his philosophic development did not begin seriously until 1896 or 1897, when he was about 50

•

years of age. But from that time onward, commencing with an abstention from liquor, meat-eating, and smoking, gradually it took the form of subversion of body to will, intense philosophic meditation, study, and literary work. . . .

In about 1899 he turned over to the writer his office and its practice, and went into the mountains of British Columbia, in the Lake Kootenay region. There he remained for about five years, living the life of a hermit in close proximity to certain mining claims in which he was interested. While there he studied mining engineering through a correspondence school, and graduated. But, it is believed, his chief purpose in leading this hermetic life was to obtain a closer philosophic view of Nature, both physical and incorporeal; and there in the wilds of British Columbia took place his greatest development in spiritual philosophy. . . .

On the return of Judge Hatch from British Columbia, he resumed the practice of law, for some time alone, but later in partnership with . . . a fellow in philosophic research.

And then came death; and the tenement he inhabited while among us, we laid away back into its native ground. And now we have his post-mortem memoirs reminding us that man has too long been satisfied with Faith, which is conviction without proof, and which has no permanent basis on which to rest, but is merely propped up by desire and longing which, being beyond present attainment, have become Hope—and Faith is only Hope realized in contemplation.

So for Judge Hatch on earth, Faith did not suffice. Like a lawyer, he sought Truth, whose basis is proof. . . .

The *Los Angeles Times* published the following eulogy to Judge Hatch shortly after his death on February 21, 1912:

A GREAT MAN

Former Judge David Patterson Hatch, who died in this city on Tuesday, was a remarkable man in many respects. While a just judge and profoundly learned in all law and practice, he was exceptionally versed in the deep philosophies of life. In these studies he had attained to a knowledge of universal law which, although natural to him, appeared as mysticism to those who had not followed his great mental strides. Many years ago he began the publication of a remarkable series of books under the Hindu name of Karishka, the most noted of these being the famous novel, *El Reshid.* This is the story of a great master of wisdom. His works on the philosophy of the Hermetics and his *Scientific Occultism* have received a wide welcome from all students in that line of thought.

274

●

Among the series of books written by Hatch under the pseudonym Paul Karishka was one called *The Twentieth Century Christ*. It was this book that brought Judge Hatch and Elsa Barker together.

Elsa Barker was born in Leicester, Vermont, in 1869. She worked as a teacher, a shorthand

reporter, a newspaper writer and an editor before achieving recognition as a poet, playwright and author. Prior to *Letters*, her books included *The Son of Mary Bethel, The Frozen Grail and Other Poems, Stories from the New Testament for Children*, and *The Book of Love* (poems), all published between 1909 and 1912. Her labor play, *The Scab*, was produced in New York City and Boston in 1904–5.

Elsa Barker

It was while writing *The Son of Mary Bethel*, the story of the Christ reborn in a modern environment, that Ms. Barker came upon an advertisement for the book *The Twentieth Century Christ*. Realizing the book had a similar theme to her own, she wrote to make inquiries and was eventually brought in touch with Judge Hatch. Their subsequent friendship lasted half a dozen years on the earth plane and led to even more significant consequences after his passing over.

Elsa Barker spent most of her life in Boston and New York, but for three years—1910–1913—she lived in Paris, and for a year after that she resided in London. In 1915, she published *Songs of a Vagrom Angel*, a book of poems she claimed came to her from the Beautiful Being described in *Letters*. In the twenties and thirties, she wrote numerous works of fiction, poetry, and magazine articles. Elsa Barker died August 21, 1954, in New York City.

BEYOND WORDS PUBLISHING, INC.

Our corporate mission

INSPIRE TO INTEGRITY

Our declared values

We give to all of life as life has given us.
We honor all relationships.
Trust and stewardship are integral
to fulfilling dreams.
Collaboration is essential to create miracles.
Creativity and aesthetics nourish the soul.
Unlimited thinking is fundamental.
Living your passion is vital.
Joy and humor open our hearts to growth.
It is important to remind ourselves of love.

Our promise to our customers

We will provide you with the highest quality books
and related products that meet or exceed your
expectations. As our customer, you will be satisfied
with your purchase and will receive your order
promptly, or we will refund your money.

•

OTHER BOOKS OF INTEREST FROM BEYOND WORDS PUBLISHING, INC.

YOU CAN HAVE IT ALL

Author: Arnold M. Patent, $16.95 hardcover

Joy, peace, abundance—these gifts of the Universe are available to each of us whenever we choose to play the *real* game of life: the game of mutual support. *You Can Have It All* is a guidebook that shows us how to move beyond our beliefs in struggle and shortage, open our hearts, and enjoy a life of true ecstasy. Arnold Patent first self-published *You Can Have It All* in 1984, and it became a classic with over 200,000 copies in print. This revised and expanded edition reflects his greater understanding of the principles and offers practical suggestions as well as simple exercises for improving the quality of our lives.

THE GREAT CHANGE

Author: White Deer of Autumn

$14.95 hardcover, $29.95 signed Author's Edition with two greeting-card prints from the book

Nine-year-old Wanba asks, " Why does anything have to die? Why did Grandpa have to die?" Grandma explains that just as a caterpillar "dies" only to become a beautiful butterfly, there is no death in the Circle of Life, only the Great Change. This is a story of passing on tradition, culture, and wisdom to the next generation. Watercolor illustrations throughout by internationally acclaimed painter Carol Grigg.

•

OTHER BOOKS OF INTEREST

QUIET PRIDE: Ageless Wisdom of the American West
Author: J. Bourge Hathaway
Photographer: Robert Alan Clayton, $39.95 hardcover

A celebration of elder Americans, this remarkable collection of photographs and narration preserves the stories, wisdom, and insight of Native and non-Native American elders. Their shared commonality is simple enough: men and women from 60 to 115 years old who chose to live their lives out West on their own terms. These are the people who live at the end of the road you never drive down. They are folks who have probably never stopped to examine their convictions because they were too busy living them. This book is about our relationship to the world, to the ones we love, to self, to our past, and most surely to our future. Printed on recycled paper using soy-based inks.

NOBLE RED MAN:
Lakota Wisdomkeeper Mathew King
Compiler and editor: Harvey Arden, $16.95 hardcover

Lakota chief and spiritual leader Noble Red Man (Mathew King) spoke with a voice so powerful that not even death could silence him. He left behind a legacy of wisdom for us to experience and ponder in this narrative compiled by the co-author of *Wisdomkeepers.* With inspiration and insight, Noble Red Man gives voice to the struggle of Native Americans and celebrates the endurance of their spirit. An heir to the traditions left by both Crazy Horse and Sitting Bull, he applies the wisdom of the Elders to everyday personal and political situations. A tribute to honor a revered chief, this book is for those interested in history as the starting place to create the future.

OTHER BOOKS OF INTEREST

WISDOMKEEPERS: Meetings with Native American Spiritual Elders
Authors: Harvey Arden and Steve Wall
Photographer: Steve Wall, $39.95 hardcover, $22.95 softcover

An extraordinary spirit-journey into the lives, minds, and natural-world philosophy of seventeen Native American spiritual Elders. They are the Old Ones, the fragile repositories of sacred ways and natural wisdom going back millennia. In the magnificent photographs and powerful words of the Wisdomkeepers, you share their innermost thoughts and feelings, their dreams and visions, their jokes and laughter, their healing remedies, and their apocalyptic prophecies. Above all, you share their humanity.

HINDSIGHTS: The Wisdom and Breakthroughs of Remarkable People
Author: Guy Kawasaki, $22.95 hardcover

What have you learned from your life that you would like to share with the next generation? Get a fresh appreciation of the human experience in this inspirational collection of interviews with thirty-three people who have overcome unique challenges. They are candid about their failures and disappointments, and insightful about turning adversity into opportunity. Guy Kawasaki spent over two years researching and interviewing such people as Apple Computer co-founder Steve Wozniak, management guru Tom Peters, and entrepreneur Mary Kay. But not everyone in the book is a celebrity. They share their revelations and life experiences, motivating the reader for both personal and professional growth.

•

OTHER BOOKS OF INTEREST

MEN, WOMEN AND RELATIONSHIPS:
Making Peace with the Opposite Sex
Author: Dr. John Gray, $12.95 softcover

From the best-selling author of *Men Are from Mars, Women Are from Venus* comes the ultimate guide for loving relationships in the '90s and beyond. Included is an examination of the strengths, needs, vulnerabilities, and mysteries unique to each sex; guidance on how to lower tensions, release resentments, and avoid misunderstandings; and strategies for successfully giving and receiving emotional support. Also available on audiotape.

RAISING A SON: Parents and the Making of a
Healthy Man
Authors: Don and Jeanne Elium, $18.95 hardcover, $12.95 softcover

This conversationally styled "how-to" book, written by family counselors, is a guide to assist both mother and father in the parts they must play in the making of a healthy, assertive, and loving man. It is suitable for parents, professional care providers, and educators. The authors consider who men are and what they need, and they are especially hard-hitting concerning Dad, who may have not understood his vital role in his son's successful masculine development. The masculine and feminine energies of fathers and mothers are realigned into a parenting partnership in this book, and single-parent strategies are also addressed.

To order or to receive a catalog, contact:
Beyond Words Publishing, Inc.
4443 NE Airport Road
Hillsboro, OR 97124-6074
503-693-8700 or 1-800-284-9673

•